I0169109

55 Rules for a Good Life:

Pursuing Truth and Responsibility

★

Brigadier General Doug Satterfield

U.S. Army (Retired)

Copyright © 2022 by

Douglas R. Satterfield.

All rights reserved.

No part of this book may be used or reproduced in any manner, electronic or mechanical, photocopying, recording or by any information storage and retrieval system, or otherwise, without written permission from the publisher, except by reviewers, who may quote brief passages in a review.

Published in the United States of America.

First Printing October 2022

Email: douglas.r.satterfield@gmail.com

Website: https://www.theLeaderMaker.com

The views expressed here are those of the author and do not reflect the official position of the U.S. Government. Stories and opinions about events here are mine, and errors are strictly my responsibility.

YL
YOUNG
LEADERS

ISBN 978-1-7379155-2-2 (paperback)

TO MY WIFE NANCY

Thank you for letting me stand with you at all times.

AND

TO MY PARENTS AND FAMILY

Thank you, mom and dad, for raising me properly. My brother and sisters for tolerating me. My grandparents for their patience and forbearance. My children for their independence. And my grandchildren that they might one day know how to be good men and women.

AND

TO MY TROOPS

Thank you for teaching me more about life than I ever could learn anywhere else.

Brigadier General Doug Satterfield is also the author of:

"Our Longest Year in Iraq," September 2021

This book is a powerful narrative of the second year of America's war in Iraq (2004-2005). In his own words, General Satterfield gives us a firsthand account of America's military build-up as our troops battled insurgents and terrorists.

From the ancient city of Ur, where Abraham lived, to the dangers of Sadr City, Baghdad, and Fallujah, construction Engineers of the 1st Cavalry Division and its 353rd Engineer Group, were there.

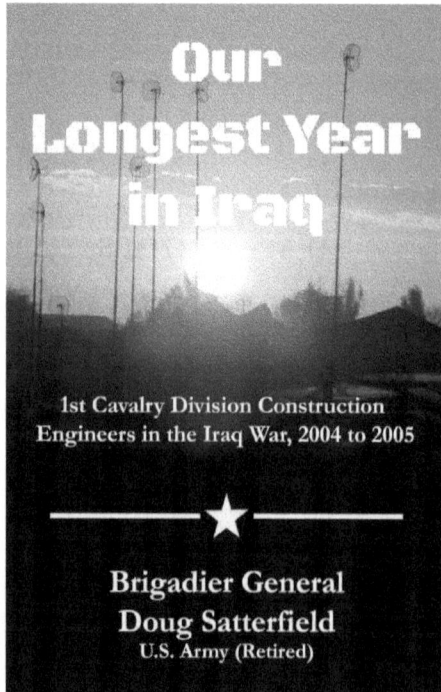

Our Longest Year in Iraq

1st Cavalry Division Construction
Engineers in the Iraq War, 2004 to 2005

★

**Brigadier General
Doug Satterfield**
U.S. Army (Retired)

55 Rules for a Good Life:

Pursuing Truth and Responsibility

Table of Contents:

"It took untold generations to get you where you are. A little gratitude might be in order."
Jordan B. Peterson

ACKNOWLEDGMENTS

Of all those who contributed, I want to thank you for making my book what it is.

I have to start by thanking my awesome wife, Nancy. She was the chief reason this book got done, from reading early drafts to giving advice on the cover to keeping the daily affairs out of my hair so I could write. Her ability to "see" through the fog of interpersonal affairs is remarkable and her insights were instrumental to this book's success. She is my go-to person, and her combined wit, mental awareness, and tenacity make her formidable.

It is said that our lives are a product of many centuries of human struggle and our own free will to make decisions, good or bad, and to follow the proper way or not. I believe this to be true. To those who came before us, I humbly salute you, for you have made our lives easier and continue to show us what is meaningful and ethical.

As an author, I relied upon the ideas of many great thinkers – philosophers, artists, entrepreneurs, religious clergy, imaginative doers, and military theorists. Creative and unbelievably thoughtful, they put into words those things we can see but are often unable to put into words ourselves. You can find their beliefs throughout this book, often in the stories that explain their thinking. They gave countless insights, and their ideas are used to underpin these 55 rules for a good life.

And from the ideas of great thinkers like Friedrich Nietzsche, Karl Jung, Aleksandr Solzhenitsyn, Jean Piaget, Erich Neumann, and Jordan Peterson, whose insight and brilliance have gotten millions worldwide to think about how to look for a good life. With their astute thinking, we've all gained a new appreciation of how to be stronger mentally and understand the strength of the human mind.

Furthermore, ordinary folks doing extraordinary things - those with dangerous jobs that provide a new dimension were most helpful; oil field workers, loggers, electrical linemen, farmers, delivery drivers, and local religious leaders. And I relied upon professional Soldiers, among the finest people America has produced. Their insights gave reason to use what they know and how to make application of those ideas. In this book, you will get more than just a peak at their thinking; you will understand what sets them apart (and you) from the ordinary and what makes them great human beings. Heroes? Yes, that's right, they are heroes of a sort because they are brave enough to seek adventure and live to tell their tales.

U.S. Army Colonel Adam Roth, a true military intellect has provided me with a common sense perspective that works. He is the kind of person who "makes things happen." I'm honored to have him on my team.

The combination of these ancient and modern thinkers gives clarity; that is what you will find throughout this book. Their contributions are there for those willing to seek out their ideas. They are outlined here for you. You will not find such a collection anywhere else. Now it is up to you.

Doug Satterfield
October 2022

FORWARD

by Adam S. Roth, U.S. Army Colonel

In his book, 55 Rules for a Good Life, Brigadier General Doug Satterfield gives us a practical view of how to have a life for yourself that you can admire. It goes something like this. Choose your yoke (Satterfield uses metaphors) and choose the weight you have to carry to justify your existence to yourself, so at the end of the day, you can look at yourself and conclude that you helped set things right. Satterfield tells a compelling and very ancient story, which is why so many people are attracted to his ideas. I know this because I know Satterfield well.

He tells us that we are given neither a good life nor a bad life; rather, it is up to us to do with it as we will. In his book, he simultaneously acts as a realist and a philosopher. He points out that the way to live well – to have a good life – is to pursue truth (and let the consequences fall as they may) and willingly adopt all the responsibility you can bear (even when doing so frightens you). His message is harsh. If your back is bent from bearing your responsibilities, he would say you are on the right path. And expect your path to be full of dragons (another of his common metaphors) that will devour you for unwise choices and do so unpredictably. Our ancestors knew this well. Through a conscious, purposeful, focused effort, we can develop ourselves and become someone who masters challenges and achieves a good life.

I find the traits exemplified most in America's "Greatest Generation" were those imbued with hardship, doing without, and, most importantly, the absolute necessity of self-responsibility. Satterfield understands this generation, and they taught him well. They spent their childhood in the Great Depression and later fought the Axis Powers in World War II, setting the moral compass for many generations. But as we got further away from those ideals, we started to erode as a society. Satterfield captured many of the "rules" this generation used to achieve some of the most remarkable feats in human history. For those lucky enough to have been raised by either parents or grandparents of the Greatest Generation, you understand.

However, the fallacy of the Greatest Generation was when fathers came home from WWII; they would tell their children that "they are working hard so you won't have to." As we look at the current state of affairs in our society, work ethics, public discourse, political divisiveness, etc., we see that as a Nation, we have lost our way because we were handed the necessities of life from our Greatest Generation.

In Satterfield's 55 Rules for a Good Life, he is able to take learning and teaching moments from the ancients and the moderns and share them with everyone wanting to better themselves. From his experiences growing up from humble beginnings to his long-time service to our Nation in the U.S. Army, and later his experiences as a father, grandfather, and husband have all been tied into concrete items that one can consider for inclusion into their own self-improvement plan.

If you have grown up mistakenly thinking that "it's all about you" and suddenly finding out in your first job, sadly, it is not the case; this book can provide new insights on how to take personal responsibility and pursue the truth required to shape your own destiny, and get on the good side of life; a life you can respect.

If you spend your life living as a victim, Satterfield's book shows you empowering concepts that can incrementally free you from your situation and help you to develop a roadmap to your own personal success.

If you find yourself not finding value in your relationships with your family, your co-workers, and your friends, or being told that you appear "selfish," "self-absorbed," or "self-serving" but don't have the context (or the tools) to be able to change that "label," Satterfield's book provides a "how to" in personal image redefinition.

If you did not grow up in a household that incorporated aunts, uncles, grandparents, and even great-grandparents who were able to provide intangible guidance to you on a regular basis and did not have the grounding to know where to start to "see what you were missing," Satterfield's book will give you a peek into those kitchen table discussions that were passed from generation to generation.

As someone who has commanded nearly a thousand Soldiers in combat, I can tell you that in my 30 years of military service, I was always looking for some way of helping the younger generation who seemed to not "get it." Often, they did not possess those life skills and life lessons needed to be a responsible individual in society (or our Army). Doug Satterfield has found a way of capturing the "secret sauce" of that older generation and their inheritance to younger generations. Doing so gives you a fighting chance in the harsh and dangerous world we find ourselves in and how to thrive.

Like the old U.S. Army recruiting slogan said, "Be all you can be." Better yet, be more than you can be.

"Give a man a fish, and he will eat for a day. Teach a man how to fish, and you feed him for a lifetime." – from an Anne Isabella Thackeray Ritchie novel 1885

INTRODUCTION

Why *55 Rules for a Good Life*? The only way to correctly answer this question is to say what I believe to be true; that everyone deserves a better existence. Yet, it's up to us to make it so. No one will hold us by the hand and lead us there.

If you are interested in making yourself a better person, getting fulfillment from life, or making a difference, this book is for you. If you are young, you are beginning your journey into adulthood. Congratulations. The fact that you are reading this book proves your desire to be better than you can be, better than you ever thought you could be.

Yes, you should be better than you are, but it's not because you're worse than other people. It's because you're not everything you should be.

To be better as a person means knowing where you're going, how to get there, and the motivation to get there. That is the key message to you and never forget it. And this is a harsh and difficult lesson; reality is unforgiving, you can be a truly good person, but you have to want it, consciously learn how to succeed and aim high enough. That is a forbidding and difficult idea.

You will struggle. That is life, to rise above tragedy and malevolence to succeed in your pursuit of a good life.

To do so, you will need a life strategy. That is what this book is about. A good analogy is driving a car to the grocery store; you need to know where the store is located, the route to get there, and a car (and how to drive it). Without all three, you are adrift, and you will suffer, become resentful, and bitter, which is not a good place to find yourself.

My message is that everyone can succeed in life, regardless of how intelligent, good-looking, or popular we are. Looking back on human history, the greatest people were not beautiful, strong, or lucky, none of these things. They were successful because they knew where they were going, how to get there, and were motivated. Only through self-motivation can you take action to live well and support your family, community and, yes, even improve upon the world. For those who reject the idea that we can make ourselves and the world better, I wish you well; this book is not for you.

I will acknowledge there is also a random element in life. Tragedies can strike us down without warning. A disaster occurs and shocks us. An illness or an accident takes us out. Moreover, what we are born with binds us as a permanent handicap (or advantage) limiting us. That is the burden we all must face.

In this book, I present to you 55 "rules" for a good life. Study them; they are proven ways to remake yourself into someone you can admire. Understanding these rules and how they can work for the good of everyone is challenging. However, it is far from impossible. Even the youngest child can recognize his limits and adjust his behavior to mimic rules that put him on the right path.

We are naturally attracted to people who show promise, demonstrate spirit, and act confidently. A positive influence in this world is about possessing those personal traits based on time-tested, ethical principles.

This book provides the most useful, no-nonsense rules for you. In all of humankind's history, we've been struggling to discover the path to being a better person, feeling more confident, and obtaining satisfaction with our lives. These rules will help you get there. And these rules are for everyone, regardless of background, age, status, race, sex, beauty, faith, privilege, personality style, or current or past circumstances.

Following these rules also means you must be willing to face your transformation. You are going to be changed. Others have done so. You can do it.

There are daily tangible actions we can take to make ourselves better. Taking those actions to the next level will make people sit up and take notice. They will begin to see you as someone they can appreciate, trust, and gravitate toward. This is worthwhile because it is how to begin your journey of good.

Today, you begin to learn the secrets of success, those essential rules I learned the hard way. I am sharing them with you now.

The choice is yours. An easy path looms ahead for those interested in today's fashion, fads, and promises of fun. For you, however, a true adventure awaits. Make a choice. Chose wisely.

The obvious question is, "Why did I write this book?" I think it was the fear of not saying what I know to be true about people, that we can be good, responsible, and honest. Ultimately, I would be a failure if I did not stand up and say what I needed to say about this inherent goodness. I had the choice to remain silent; I chose not to.

This is what life is about – pursuing truth and responsibility. That is the path to a good life, a meaningful life.

"There is nothing noble in being superior to our fellow man; true nobility is being superior to your former self." – Ernest Hemingway

★ RULE 1

Realize that nobody owes you nuttin'. Not only does no one owe you anything, you owe the world everything. Once you accept this truth, you will be forever free to pursue your future as you wish.

It's never too late to start.

Most of us grew up under the watchful eye of our mothers. We quickly learned some simple rules in "her" house. "I'm not your maid." "Get your butt in here, now!" "Elbows off the table." "Don't do anything stupid." And, "Nobody owes you nuttin'." If you wanted to eat breakfast, have a cookie, or have fun outside with your friends, you first had to follow the rules and do a few chores. This included helping do the laundry, clearing out wasp nests (my favorite), making the bed, taking out the trash, and sweeping the house. Both boys and girls, no one was exempt, and there were high expectations. You followed the rules, or else! There were no safe spaces or trophies for trying. You quickly learned to follow the rules.

"Realize that nobody owes you nuttin" is one of the most valuable rules of life because it sets the conditions for everything else we do. Orient yourself to this idea and your world will instantly look brighter. You can only be free if you give up on the idea that people owe you something. It may seem corny to point this out, but there is no free lunch. Someone pays. Most of us have figured this out; taking a handout makes you beholden. I didn't like that one bit, and neither should you.

We are bombarded with television, movies, and social media that tell us we are worthy people and entitled to live a prosperous, healthy, and wonderful life where we are beautiful, have great careers, get free education, and have a low-stress, comfortable life. Unfortunately, they are teaching us terrible life lessons. And not only are they wrong, but they are helping create a generation of people who are routinely disappointed and unhappy because they didn't get what they "deserved."

Politicians are first in line to tell us that we are owed something just because. Just because we are alive, or we are citizens, or we meet their definition of a particular victim group. We are told if you want it, you should have it. It's your right, they tell us. It's a fact that all those folks who line up to get their goodies will inevitably leave disappointed.

This disappointment turns to bitterness and resentment. Those same people who tell us we are entitled are the ones who also tell us we are victims and now deserve some form of government assistance or compensation for the unfairness of life. That pity party never stops, and the results are awful; high suicide rates, increased crime, random muggings and violence against people. Bitterness and resentment are a negative feedback loop that repeats without end.

Count your blessings. People don't owe you a lovely home, an education, fashionable clothes, a modern cell phone, good health, or immunity from tragedy. And it's a good thing that is not so. Perhaps our government does owe us some level of blind justice and safety, but it is up to us all to work hard together to bring this about as a reality. My cousin Billy (not his real name) still believes the government is chalked full of experts who have all the answers. After High School, he moved into his grandmom's trailer. One day, this little muscle-free child adult, sporting the obligatory mullet haircut, asked with tears in his eyes and a choking voice, "The gubmint, they take care of youse, right?" It's an infectious attitude, and there is no honorable life relying on the government. Billy still lives in a trailer.

Nobody owes you nuttin'.

"Life is hard. Life is difficult. Life is going to punch you in the gut. But when you change your attitude, you change your behavior. When your behavior changes, so do your results."
– Will Hurd

⭐ **RULE 2**

Get used to cold showers; life is tough. When we accept that life has its ups and downs, we can start to live with a better conscience. You are not safe by ignoring the danger.

Your perspective changes when you are in charge of yourself (and perhaps in charge of others) and responsible for your own well-being and accountability. You become more focused and direct and you don't take bullcrap from nobody. Life is like taking a cold shower; shocking and uncomfortable. Life can be painful. Life is tough. Life is full of tragedy. And if you're stupid and lazy and willfully blind, it's even harder. To be content with your own life, you must see life for what it is. The sooner you learn that life is tough, you can learn how to transcend those difficulties. By taking the noble path, you will realize that a life lived properly is the way to a good life. This book is about that very idea.

Part of your adult development is acknowledging and then accepting the inner strength necessary to survive. This strength is the Lion within you; strong, attentive, far-seeing, and enduring, but also brutal, dangerous, lethal, and daring. Dangerous traits are what you use to overcome the tragedies in life. Do not reject these traits (yes, they could lead you down the wrong path) but transform them for your use. You can see people who have done so and people who have not. Those who have failed to accept their dangerous side are naïve and ignorant. You can tell who they are by looking at and talking to them. And these same people are often resentful because other people take advantage of them. A dangerous person is one who has accepted and controls that inner Lion and is the one who can protect others against the inevitable perils in life.

Those who properly direct their dangerous side, just like the trained Special Forces soldier who keeps his weapon at the ready and is capable of fending off evil and hazards. Your potential for destruction is necessary. It's a persona that gives people self-respect, like the kind of respect we have for a wild animal. To control our dangerous side is to prevent rage, anger, and bitterness from overwhelming us. Either you are dangerous or not. There is no in-between. You are not safe by rejecting the danger.

Attend to your poster. Quit drooping and hunching over. Speak your mind. Put your desires forward. Walk tall and gaze forthrightly ahead. Dare to be dangerous. That is how you adapt to a perilous world.

"A cadet will not lie, cheat, steal, or tolerate those who do." –
U.S. Military Academy Cadet Honor Code

★ RULE 3

Never Lie, Cheat, or Steal. And do not needlessly tolerate those who do. The most fundamental bond among humans since the beginning of time is trust. When we lie, cheat, or steal, we break that bond. We are betraying others, and we are corrupting ourselves in the process. You will lose the race to success if you lie, cheat, or steal. Never, ever betray your brothers (or sisters).

Here's a little secret most people are hesitant to tell you. Never lie, cheat, or steal ... and do not needlessly tolerate those who do. Trust is a building block to success and a satisfying life. Of all the things I write about in this book, stopping yourself from lying, cheating, and stealing will be the most difficult to do. Those behaviors corrupt us, make us weaker, less respected, and turn us into sniveling cowards.

Telling the truth and not cheating or stealing requires practice, practice, and more practice. It is easy to slip up. We are often actively encouraged to lie, cheat, and steal by friends, family, at school, and at work. Sometimes we are taught how to do it and "get away with it." You can even lie to yourself that you are doing yourself a big favor. Or it's a way to retaliate against an unfair world. But, in the long run, you can never get away with it. Moreover, you will pay a high price.

Telling the truth is the real key. Tell the truth, or at least do not lie. Do not say those things you know to be false. Now that is an adventure.

We all know the difference between lying and telling the truth. We all know when we lie – to consciously tell someone what we know to be false. A lie is very enticing. It gives us short-term relief or prestige or gets us out of a jam. Don't do it. You will garner more respect for yourself by telling the truth, and people will go to you as someone they can trust. Tell the truth and do so even when you know that it will harm you.

The problem with lying is that it's a real hydra. Kids find this out quickly. They will tell one lie, which has one of the consequences they expected; maybe they even got away with it. But it has three or four other consequences that they don't expect. And the lie grows. Then they have to tack a lie on each of those little complexities it congers up. And the complexities grow, and this little lie turns into a great big ball of lies. At some point, the lie becomes painfully evident to everyone.

Lying also corrupts. It weakens your character. You are not standing up for yourself when you lie. You betray yourself if you say untrue things. You will no longer be capable of trusting yourself to do the right thing. When adversity comes, and make no mistake about it, adversity will come; it will destroy you when it appears because you cannot trust yourself to have the proper solution.

As a young boy picking cotton on granddaddy's farm, I put a couple of large rocks into my cotton sack. Since pickers were paid by the weight of the cotton, this was a fast way to get more money for less work. But, like so often happens, they caught me red-handed. Shame was the least of it, not that I cheated so much but as letting down my grandfather and the other workers. This incident was a significant moment in realizing it is better to be perceived by others as stupid, lazy, or weak than dishonest; someone who betrays others has no true friends.

Friedrich Nietzsche once said that a man's worth is determined by how much truth he can tolerate. Deception, flattering, lying and cheating, talking behind the back, posing, living in borrowed splendor, and taking on a false role; are what a good person is expected to reject. Truth, however, has its own struggles. Don't be a nice person, be a good person. Niceness is the idea that being untruthful to protect feelings, not telling people what you want, and avoiding all conflict, even when necessary, is all okay. Being a good person is to tell the truth, assert yourself ethically, and treat people with respect and care based on truth. This place is where the most incredible people are found.

Never, ever lie, cheat, or steal; your life depends upon it.

"Do, or do not. There is no try." – *Yoda*

★ **RULE 4**

Aim High and find your mission in life. If one thing in life is certain, you don't get something you don't aim at. Some folks will fail to specify their goals because it is "too hard" or unpleasant. Having clear goals is to have standards that specify what a failure is and what a success is. Better to aim for a noble goal.

One of the certainties in life is that you don't get something if you don't aim at it, like the Olympic archer who hits the bulls-eye only when aiming correctly. Surprisingly, many folks are reluctant to make their personal goals clear; that way, they do not have to talk about or face failure. They will never know, nor want to know, about their failures, which is okay because they would rather deny failure than face it with courage.

It is common practice to fail to aim at proper life goals. This failure means random wandering in your life that will not move you forward. Instead, it will disappoint and frustrate you, make you anxious and unhappy and hard to get along with, and then make you resentful, vengeful, and worse. Taking the easy road will not work.

Those who want meaning in their lives and seek fulfillment – the good life – should look to make their goals sharp and clear. And they should best aim high for that which is worthy and challenging to achieve. Yes, we can have several aims. One high aim could simply be to become a good person. Of course, there is more detail to this aim. Perhaps we want to reduce our distrust of others, restrain our evil thoughts, or decrease suffering, all commendable tasks. This is where we could do the most good for our family, friends, and community. Once we prove ourselves capable of being good, we can then help others achieve good in their lives.

As we keep our proper goals in our sights, we must also orient our everyday efforts toward this goal. In pursuit of a high goal – a noble goal – our day-to-day acts give our lives true meaning. That is the dignity of being human; doing so ensures we stay on the right path. Furthermore, we can judge our actions by connecting our smaller goals (or tasks) to our honorable aim.

Who do you want to be? Having a reasonable, noble aim is one of those secrets. Life has many pitfalls, and identifying the direction you want to go next week, next month, and at least three to five years down the line is an early step in the right direction. This means caring for yourself at the most basic level. Physical and mental fitness is not to be ignored.

Inexperienced and undisciplined young folks often cannot see the world clearly, and adopt oversimplified, popular life strategies that do not work. For starters, they don't take responsibility for themselves, their behavior, or their family, or they are not looking at how they could contribute to their community. And they don't understand that they don't know much, being young and inexperienced. One day they may realize that what they do is wrong for them and others. If they come to this realization, they can then take action to stop and fix themselves, but only if people put their minds to it.

And, if they seek happiness as their goal, they are not aiming properly. Happiness is not one of the goals we should pursue. First, happiness is not a noble aim. Happiness occurs almost randomly; it comes and goes, and we should appreciate it when it comes. But happiness is fleeting and unpredictable. If you want happiness, drink alcohol and abuse drugs (that's a bit of sarcasm). But drug use works, at least in the short term, and it's cheap and instantaneous. Of course, alcohol and many drugs destroy the lives of perhaps five to ten percent of our society and severely handicap those it does not kill.

Don't pursue happiness. Pursue who you could be because you are not who you could be, and you know it. We lack the proper discipline; we procrastinate; we are complacent; we have bad habits and odd tastes; we are self-righteous; we do things that make no sense. We know perfectly well that we are not who we could be. Do those things that are good and will benefit others. Do this by developing your character as much as possible. And maybe, just maybe, if you are lucky, happiness will descend upon you on occasion. You can be grateful for that brief happiness. That is the best that we've got.

Improve your character. Be the adult in the room. Adopt discipline; stop doing those things you know you should not be doing, do those things you know you should do and stop chasing happiness. We don't judge a person by the size of their house, the clothes they wear, or the music they listen to, but by whether that person has character. Regardless of your circumstances, the first thing you can do is learn to deal with those things you can fix. After that, the world is open. That is one measure of character.

Aim high for a noble goal because you will never live a good life without doing so.

"If you don't ask, you don't get." — Stevie Wonder

★ **RULE 5**

Find someone to help you paddle. There is a universal truth that tells us that you cannot change yourself without help. Find someone who has your interests at heart and ask them to assist you. It takes a spouse, friends, colleagues, and sometimes a stranger to guide you to the right destination.

There is an old U.S. Navy saying that when you get a mission, "Find someone to help you paddle." You need others to help you complete your tasks or fulfill your mission! While this may seem unfashionable as an idea, we all know that going it alone does not work. Old western movies show the "lone cowboy" who rides his faithful horse to the rescue, chases off the bad guys, saves the damsel in distress and returns the stolen stagecoach gold. That's not the way the world works. Even the hero needs help.

Ask someone to do you a favor so that you can return it. You may not be able to change the world, but you can make a significant impact. You cannot do this alone, without people standing with you. Asking someone for a favor is the beginning of building trust. Nurture this trust by building a network of friends and acquaintances you can rely on. Humans learned long ago that we could do nothing of consequence without others.

"Doug, if your guys are in trouble, just call, and we will be there." This particular Infantry Battalion Commander was a man of his word. We were all American Soldiers, and we protected our own. If there was an attack on one of our reconnaissance convoys or patrols, we were to call him. He would send his forces to get us out of a jam no matter his current mission, no matter what. These Soldiers would do anything in their power to save our butts, and that is the environment we were to appreciate. What a great feeling to know others would help us no matter the circumstances; they had our back.

With others at our side, outstanding achievements can take place. It may be the older man who empties the trashcan or the senior vice president who gives you a chance to excel; we all play a role in the success of others. Never forget them, no matter their job or status. Do your best to help them as well. Treat them with dignity and respect. Judge them for their character. You will gain much from those reciprocal relationships in proportion to the effort you also put into them.

Be part of the team. Whether in the workplace, at home with your family, as a player on a sports team, or just having fun with friends, achieving the team's goals requires working together cooperatively. We call it teamwork, which means understanding your role, listening to what others say, and holding yourself accountable for your mistakes. It's incredible how easy it is to be a team player, but it does require commitment and staying power. "Hey, coach, put us in the game. I want to play." Now, that is the right attitude.

Writers of the Bible, ancient philosophers and other thinkers of the past had it right about reality. "Ask, and it shall be given to you, seek, and ye shall find, knock and it shall be opened unto you." If you are willing to be part of your community and have the courage to ask for what you need, you will get it. If you are present and paying attention, and you are looking for opportunities, they will find you.

Opportunity knocks, but only if you are willing to approach the door and be a willing participant. Social scientists long ago discovered that if you don't try to accomplish anything, you will never succeed. Free handouts don't exist. Undoubtedly, it requires foresight and conscious effort on your part. Be willing to seek what you need. Begin today.

Imagine, if you will, what you would like your life to be like a few years from now. Picture what you could have, reasonably, and what you could do to get there in your mind. Then ask what the requirements are for it to be so. Ask what the conditions of success are to see what is needed to succeed. Do not hide in your room. Nothing ever will be accomplished from your willful blindness. Some folks are reluctant to look ahead to their future, and by failing to look ahead, they are less likely to succeed. They have no way of measuring if they are on the right track because they don't know their end goal.

Figure out what you would like to be. Then aim for it carefully and single-mindedly. And ask for help, and others will help you. If you do this, you will succeed; that success may not be straightforward or immediate, but it will happen.

Find someone to help you paddle.

"If you know the enemy and know yourself, you need not fear the results of a hundred battles." – Sun Tzu

★ **RULE 6**

Know Yourself, Know your Troops, Know your Enemy; this is the mark of a mature individual.
Know your weaknesses, and never forget.
Know your troops, and you will always overcome danger.
Know your enemy, and you will win every battle.

KNOW YOURSELF:

The Greeks had a maxim, "Know thyself." This idea was not new in the time of the Greeks because it was an incredibly ancient way of thinking. The importance of knowing yourself as the basis of a high-quality and balanced life goes back into the darkness of human antiquity. It is a story that repeatedly resonates. Why? Because it's true.

In terms of personality and potential, how do we come to know ourselves? The first way to understand yourself is to understand what you do not understand. With practice, you can learn to observe your behavior like that of a stranger. However, to do this, you must have a form of extreme humility. There are two sources to this humility: recognizing your ignorance and understanding your potential. Take great care and think about what you do that makes you better, and then ask yourself what habits you have that hurt you.

You will discover a little about your potential as you discover who you are and whether your habits serve your purpose. You will also discover the darker, dangerous (or evil) part of yourself. There's some utility in knowing your potential for mayhem and destruction. It is essential to realize how to incorporate that dangerous part of yourself into a higher-order personality since only by doing so will it make you unstoppable. This is how you become a Lion among others.

The other thing you can do to discover yourself is to challenge yourself. Look at what you could and how you should improve yourself (even if it is very small) by your standards. Set yourself some small goals to start and take them on. Then take larger and more significant challenges. But, begin incrementally, with small steps. Over time, your efforts will grow exponentially, and you will soon see the payoff.

Start now, and do not be overwhelmed. Everyone starts when they're ignorant and biased and deeply flawed and immature. Challenge yourself continually to see how far past yesterday you can push today and tomorrow. Repeatedly experiment with expanding the areas of your competence and your ability to increase that competence.

The upper limit you can achieve depends on the effort you put into it. The more it's accompanied by truth, speech, and action, the more you will develop your potential, truly a voluntary adventure. Such actions will take you from the ordinary and propel you into a more stable, resilient, reliable, and stalwart being. There is nothing better you can do for yourself.

KNOW YOUR TROOPS:

We read those stories of our heroes' brave deeds, those who put their lives on the line for others in displays of unbelievable courage. We need good citizens like that, and for reasons of necessity, we do indeed love our heroes. But there are also many more stories of ordinary folks who, along with their teammates, accomplish unimaginable feats. Know your troops, their stories, their quirks and their minds, their needs and wants, their fears and their courage. Know those who work for you. Know your peers and those who you surround yourself with. Together you can achieve more than even your imagination can see. Surrounding yourself with good people is no easy task, but if you do, you will see what you've never seen before; an incredibly good life.

I began my time in the U.S. Army as a Private, the lowest rank; I was a simple foot Soldier. Over the years, I learned much from America's best Sergeants in charge of us. There was something important to take from that experience. In early assignments as an army Private, we would experience some tough lessons in the Army. We all wanted to know more and be more like those Sergeants. We learned that to do what's right with our team meant you had to have the right people and leaders to make it happen.

Years later, when promoted to the rank of "buck" Sergeant, experiences as a Private led me to swear that I would never give up on them and never let them down. It was easy to empathize with what they had to endure. If you've been one of them, gotten dirty, scared, exhausted, survived the fight, and took on all comers, they respected that fact. It is necessary to pay your dues. Relevant experience works but the road to get there was no picnic. Physical and mental scars proved we were willing to lock shields with our Battle Buddies and never give up on them. To this day, we remain tied together through the strongest of bonds; we are Brothers.

Many troops today, especially those in the most senior positions, have forgotten the foot Soldier. Leaders ps are caught up in the affairs of their job, the daily emails, the meetings, the workshops, getting that corner office, going out to lunch with their boss, and even rubbing elbows with politicians. With each passing day, their distance from the troops grows. And it grows to such an extent they no longer wish to be associated with the ordinary troop. It happens too many times. And it's happening today in our political senior military leaders as they adopt simple ideologies over military preparedness. Many now say that our military readiness is declining due to this corruption; all the while, our leaders grow arrogant and selfish.

This philosophy demands we get to know our troops. It works!

Know your troops, for this is the only way to become part of the bond of brotherhood. And this is the only way to be truly successful.

KNOW THE ENEMY:

Never underestimate your enemy. The "enemy" symbolically refers to people opposed to you, those with competing ideas, desires, and missions. They could be an opposing army, a terrorist group, a strongman dictator who wants to destroy the world, or the metaphysical Devil. The enemy can be as tiny as a drunk friend trying to drive his car home after a binge of alcohol or great as a foreign nation's tyrant running a country and planning to do your nation great harm.

"Know your enemy" was a maxim before recorded history. Failure to know your enemy could very well lead to your death and, as well, a Darwinian demise of those around you. In the business world, a related axiom is "Never underestimate the competition." When we underestimate the enemy, people suffer – massacres, genocides, and holocausts occur and bring untold misery. Historical events of the previous few centuries still reverberate throughout our social fabric. Many of the twentieth century's horrific deaths are there for seeing; the world miscalculated Stalin, Hitler, Mussolini, and Mao. Learn about your enemy. Learn about evil.

Combined with fear and the lack of moral courage, failure to know your enemy will lead to the expansion of evil. Not maybe;

if you don't know the enemy, a dangerous game is being played. Today, we see the worldwide growth of terror, the crushing of ideas, the rejection of Judaism and Christendom, and the labeling free speech as evil. Our response has been timid, underwhelming, and restricted mainly to the West. An enemy is destroyed through strength and courage, never through acquiescence or appeasement.

To know your enemy, you must – at least symbolically – become your enemy. The surviving texts from the ancient world tell of a Chinese General named Sun Tzu. He wrote more than two millennia ago, "To know your enemy, you must become your enemy." He tells us to put ourselves in the position of our enemies so that we can understand and predict his actions. Know his strengths and weaknesses, learn his strategies and tactics, and hold his core ideas close; that is how you can see what he will do next. Learn his behavior patterns, what he hungers for, where he is weak and strong, and his values and virtues. Knowing these are your path to victory.

Never underestimate your enemy. This means knowing your enemy but also knowing yourself and your troops. Only then can you win.

"Be Prepared." — the Boy Scout Motto

★ **RULE 7**

Wear your helmet, clean your rifle, and carry a rucksack. Be like the Boy Scouts and be prepared for those unforeseen problems. Life occasionally throws us a curveball and surprises us. That way, you are ready, and you will come out stronger than before.

Working with Boy Scouts as an adult leader is a satisfying and distinctive experience. Each day, I could see in those young boys what I was like at their tender age; gullible, fragile, unfocused, and often fearful, yet also funny, curious, free-spirited, adventurous, and open. It was up to us, the scout adult leaders, to teach them how to be prepared.

Every summer camp, we would spend an entire week living out in the woods. In those unforgettable times, adult leaders would see young boys growing up and growing up fast. Soon to be men, our boys would spend much of their time in the water swimming, canoeing, rafting, playing water games, and learning to rescue people from drowning. Such adventures are a path to learning essential life skills. One day they will need those skills; besides, it's fun to participate in and entertaining to watch.

While attending summer camp, leaders give advice to make the boy's stay outdoors easier, giving them a few secrets as they learn the field craft necessary. For example, we let them know that wearing their swimming trunks all day will cause irritation between their legs. It is easy for a young boy not to listen; changing clothes several times during the day is "inconvenient." Each summer camp week, several of the youngest scouts completely ignored us (although they would surely deny doing so). After a few days, they walk bow-legged around our campsite. "Who are you, John Wayne?" our Scout Master would ask. A few of the youngest boys did not understand the reference to the days of the Old West; that was okay. We brought several large containers of medicated powder to camp for their use. They learned the hard way (a good way to remember, but the hard way has its pitfalls), but listening to the advice of others with more experience and foresight is much easier.

As a Boy Scout, I also worked for a local farmer. His advice about life and work stuck with me. Several of us worked outside caring for his dairy cattle. He said to wear proper clothing and footwear, carefully clean and maintain his tools, learn how to use them safely, and always carry a large folding knife and a 20-foot rope. It was the rubber boots that made the difference. Ignoring his advice the first day and stepping in a foot of wet mud infused with cow manure does not go well with sneakers. On the upside, his daughter was beautiful. No surprise; I worked there for several summers.

By the time my friends and I joined the U.S. Army, we were ready to be Soldiers (or at least we thought). Our next-door farmer had taught his employees a lot (especially about cleanliness and attention to detail). He made it easier on us later in life when the Drill Sergeants taught us newbie recruits to properly clean and maintain our rifles. To those Sergeants, this was the most important thing to know, along with teaching us that your weapon is your best friend. The farmer and the Soldier have much in common if they are not adequately prepared, hell is on the way.

We were also trained to use proper fieldcraft; to correctly wear our helmets (there is a wrong way), proper camouflage techniques, and what to take along in a rucksack (extra ammo, a poncho, a spare pair of socks, a t-shirt, toiletries, and duct tape) — nothing else. Those scruffy Drill Sergeants were combat veterans from the Vietnam War and had the experience and knowledge. They survived the war and wanted to ensure we did not make the same deadly mistakes, so many of them and their friends had made in combat (and never returned). Their Soldier lessons were learned the hard way too. They were prepared. We wanted to be just like them; rough, ready, and deadly. Be like the Boy Scouts, be prepared.

Wear your helmet, clean your rifle, and carry your rucksack. Be prepared. Or else!

"Know how to listen, and you will profit even from those who talk badly." – Plutarch

★ **RULE 8**

Listen intently to others because they might know something you don't. And listen especially to your enemies; they will tell you what they are about to do.

Listening is a lost art. I'll be blunt; we are terrible listeners. That means everybody, not just your family or your best friend; you too are a lousy listener. Today's young adults are worst at listening than any generation. Young men are the worst. The sooner we recognize this as a problem, the sooner we will take action to be better listeners.

That is unfortunate because we now have to work harder with our self-inflicted "don't listen" mental handicap. That problem prevents us from learning about who were are and how others see us. It stops us from learning about our family and friends. It slows our ability to get along with strangers, co-workers, and people we encounter wherever we go and whatever we do. It leads to unexpected and unproductive social relationships. It destroys commercial transactions. And it has historically led to some of the most destructive wars in human history.

Better listening builds trust, broadens your perspective, strengthens your patience, makes you approachable, saves time and money, and helps detect and resolve problems faster and cheaper. Excellent listening skills produce more competent workers, friends and family are more friendly, and our lives are more manageable. Why don't we all push ourselves to learn the basic tenets of listening? We seem to overestimate ourselves naturally and underestimate others, and that friction slows us down, but we can overcome that deficit by practicing some basic yet proven techniques. If what we do does not work, try something that is not being tried, or at least be serious about finding out what others are thinking.

Let's face it; listening is hard. However, we can do a better job with a careful and deliberate effort. There is no downside to being a better listener. And while this does not come easy, quickly, or cheaply, the payoff is substantial, more than we might believe.

For this book, why we are such poor listeners are inconsequential. We know we don't listen properly, so just admit it and learn to fix that weakness. Psychologists have long discussed the many reasons for poor listening: we are in a hurry, want to be liked, or aren't trained to listen.

Here are a few favorite techniques for listening more effectively. We all can do better. I like to think of social skills as a work-in-progress; be motivated to listen and learn. Work is the operative term; it takes time, focus, and effort.

My best advice is to slow down. Let the other person talk. Allow folks to have their say, and don't interrupt. And don't think about how you will respond with your solution or comment. Simultaneously listening and formulating a response will put you back in the same place we are all in; a terrible listener.

Some listening techniques are simple. Look people in the eye, ask questions, don't interrupt or cut them off, look for non-verbal cues, and give thoughtful feedback. Other techniques require a greater attention level. Try to understand what that other person is thinking, rephrase their words and ask if you have expressed their idea correctly to their satisfaction, and remain focused and not distracted by the daily details of life.

Active listening can help build relationships, solve problems, ensure understanding and avoid conflict. By being a better listener, we can improve our own lives and the lives of others.

Is the solution simple? No! Listening is hard for real-world reasons. We are told 24/7 that we are the best there is, we are the cat's meow, and we are a winner in all we do, and if we don't finish first, we are somehow cheated. Such talk builds an incredibly fragile foundation for adulthood. We are self-centric, and we want our way, and we want it now. Watch any television commercial; it's all there. The first step is to recognize our failure to listen correctly and then have the motivation to fix ourselves. Don't worry about the other guy; for now, convince yourself that he has something that you might actually need.

By the way, your enemies are listening and observing you. You should listen closely to them. Only by listening to them will you learn what they're up to. You just might want to know.

"Be all you can be." – *U.S. Army slogan, 1980 to 2001*

★ RULE 9

Be more than you can be. Do not just accept who you are. You could be much more than you think you could ever be.

"Just accept yourself!" Nope. Wrong. Whatever you think you can be, you can do much better. Don't just accept yourself. In other words, good enough is just not good enough.

I met Drill Sergeant S. B. Bryant shortly after joining the U.S. Army. The introduction to Sergeant Bryant was not a happy one for the 35 recruits in "his" Basic Combat Training platoon. We were about to learn that it takes more than intelligence and physical strength to be a good person, to be satisfied with life, or to be someone others look up to as credible. I was not too fond of Sergeant Bryant because I saw him as an arrogant jerk, and he made our lives miserable, but he showed us newbies how to be real Soldiers, and he was going to show us much more than we thought possible.

For me, the Army was an introduction to a new existence. The military experience shows us an element of humanness can even transcend the intellect. The Army also teaches us ways to understand people and that we are poorly adapted to using tools (weapons, armored vehicles, and such). Most importantly, under Sergeant Bryant's ever-present glare, I learned that I could be more than I thought I could ever be. He pushed us. Every day he pushed and shoved until the slowest of learners came to appreciate his all-important message that we are much more than we thought.

In the military, you learn to live up to your "potential." This philosophy has driven our life ever since; we can improve our future selves and do so consciously and voluntarily. Joining the Army was a way that allowed us to find out that we could be more than ordinary. Like so many others, we learned this lesson often the hard way. Our lessons would stick with us. Some of us cried! Some went AWOL. Some cracked. We all got stronger and more motivated and learned that sometimes even our feelings stood in the way of making us better.

Laying on his desk in his office, located at the back of our wooden barracks, was a book titled "I'm Okay, You're Okay." Published in 1967. This self-help book by psychiatrist Thomas Harris was a best seller on the New York Times book list in 1972. Sergeant Bryant had several of us standing at attention in front of him, and he spent five minutes screaming at us for doing something stupid (I can't remember what it was). He picks up the book and says, "Satterfield, you ain't okay because you gonna be a Soldier." He also screamed a few unprintable words. We were scared to death and honestly did not understand his point. Maybe we were too scared, certainly not thinking straight.

Many years later, I was walking through the massive Atlanta, Georgia airport when I stopped to buy a book to read. On the discount table was that same book, "I'm Okay, You're Okay." Sergeant Bryant's message clicked. Yeah, I'd finally figured out what he meant. He wanted "his" platoon to push beyond the impossible. Being okay just didn't cut it. If he said, "Attack that hill," we would do so without hesitation, and we would win. In battle, if you hesitate, you die, or others die. Too many people are satisfied with their current station in life or are afraid to make improvements. Sergeant Bryant made us better and convinced us that we had the power to do so ourselves.

He also said something else that was profound. And I'm paraphrasing here because I cannot remember his exact words, but it went something like this, "How can you expect to be a good Soldier when you cannot even make your bunk correctly." I always wondered what making a bed has to do with good soldiering. The answer is that people cannot be successful if they cannot order their minds properly. You begin that process by doing the small daily things you must do. Mundane things are not trivial. If you cannot order small things correctly, you will suffer terribly, and you will not be capable of fixing larger problems. Making our bunks early each morning, military style, was the first small step to getting our minds in order. Start very small, and then work up to the big problems.

I learned that the goal of life is not drinking beer on the beach and watching the waves roll in. This behavior will only make you happy for a day before you tire of it. You surely will not live up to your potential doing so. A proper goal in life can be to fix yourself, and in that way, you will not be a burden on your family or community or your Army unit. Thanks, Sergeant Bryant, for trashing that beach idea.

Years later, en route from my home in West Texas, I passed through Fort Polk, Louisiana, where Sergeant Bryant was still stationed. I arrived at the post with two friends in tow – best pals from High School. Of course, we all wanted to see this great man, the same man who wanted us to be better than "those dumbass civilians." He was a lot of fun. It turns out that entertaining times are guaranteed if you know Bryant. He was sidesplittingly funny. Sergeant Bryant helped mold us into real men and accomplished Soldiers.

"Talent wins games, but teamwork and intelligence wins championships." – Michael Jordan

★ **RULE 10**

Hold the team guidon. Be a team player.

Guys and gals of a recent generation grew up when Western movies were all the rage. The plots were usually the same; a wagon train headed West is attacked by Indians, and the Army Cavalry comes to the rescue. There was plenty of action as the Cavalry chased off the attackers. The red and white guidon (flag) was always present, with the troopers representing the rescuing Cavalry unit.

Holding the guidon is an old tradition dating back many centuries. A new, incoming leader takes the guidon (or something of similar symbolic value) from the outgoing leader. When the guidon is handed from one leader to another, so does all responsibility and accountability. The symbolism is time-honored and is taken seriously by all.

Holding the guidon can also mean taking the initiative, grabbing responsibility, or charging into battle. If you are a team player, there are times when you are expected to take the guidon. As a member, you are responsible for what does or does not happen from that moment forward. Zero excuses are accepted for failure, none. As a leader, you must look to the future and prepare your troops (or civilians) for all contingencies. It means voluntarily accepting complete responsibility for the organization, ensuring a productive association of its members, caring for them by providing for their needs, and, importantly, a formal obligation to act within their lawful authority.

Taking the guidon also symbolizes the moral and legal obligations specified in that group. The "guidon" in a civilian organization might not be a physical flag like the one we see in the military. For the King, it is his crown. For a court judge, it is a gavel. And for the CEO, it could be a large office. Those in possession of the "guidon" are the publically recognized player, someone who is in the game, upholds the values and rules of the game, and whose very presence is expected and demanded. That is always a place of honor.

Great care is observed when a new person takes the guidon. Because the fate of the team depends on the skills of that team member and their ability to work closely with other players, their dedication and voluntary loyalty are not taken lightly. Members new to the team must prove themselves and undergo an initiation period that provides them with an opportunity to show they have the right stuff and possess the moral fortitude to be a player. Someday, they might be asked to carry the guidon; their behavior today matters and is informally noted.

There's an old saying from the days of ancient Rome that ordinary foot soldiers would interconnect (or lock) their shields together for mutual defense. "Lock shields!" was the command. There's a scene in the movie "Troy" (2004) where actor Brad Pitt's warriors lock their shields during one of their attacks against the Greeks. Going into battle alone is an irrational idea. Alone, by yourself, when the arrows are flying past you, is enough to send the strongest warrior to flight.

But when you see the back of your brother's shields to your left and right, you know there is a strength that comes from it. You are not fighting alone.

Call it holding the guidon, locking shields, or being there for the team; being a team player is the ultimate in the human experience. Be part of the team if you want to be successful. Hold the team guidon.

OUTTAKE: A "no-brainer" decision

That day, the senior NCO on duty gave me a simple choice. I was transitioning out of the U.S. Army as an enlisted man, and it was August, a very hot and sweltering day. I could see Soldiers outside mowing the grass, cleaning up the sizeable grassy parade field next to the large building where I sat. I could see the sweat pouring off those young men, clearly uncomfortable out in the heat of midday. "You can go to interview with our National Guard representative, or you can help outside with the grass." As we say in the military, "It is a no-brainer decision."

I don't remember his name or much about the Guard NCO that day, nor did I try. I was interested in getting the heck out of the Army and returning to college, where I was accepted just a few months before my discharge. I remember sitting in his air-conditioned office listening to a sales pitch on joining the Guard. Previously, my active duty Commander had tried to talk me into staying in the Army; nope! I was getting out. I'd heard the dog and pony show many times before. My mind strayed. I thought about how I would be bored, once again, much as I had often been in the past. Another hurry up and wait chapter in the Army; I was used to it. Sit there, look interested, don't fidget, occasionally smile, and be polite if necessary.

I was about to enter into an important and surprisingly thoughtful conversation. Now, I was no fool, nor was I inexperienced in the ways of the Army or combat. I was in the Army for nearly seven years and had earned my spurs in some scary circumstances. I'd learned that it matters not who you are or how much experience you have; you can still screw up, be halted by fear, and get your men killed.

I would listen. The National Guard NCO asked me about my college plans and what I wanted to do after graduating [a classic sales line]. I had a vision for my life and was willing to overcome any obstacle to get my degree. Nothing would stop me, and a Guard position in the same uniform I was already wearing was not part of my plan. I already knew that I might fail out of college or fate might do me in. But I was willing to give it my best.

The Guard NCO started talking about his kids [another classic sales line] and raising kids and how being in the Guard would not interfere. I was unmarried and had no children. He said that life is difficult and you cannot always protect your children. All you can do is prepare them [yep!]. Then he said something that made sense and got my attention. I'm re-phrasing a bit, but he said something like this:

We in the National Guard have a mission to respond to natural disasters like hurricanes that recently devastated southern Louisiana. New Orleans, Louisiana, has been a particularly troublesome spot when hurricanes strike, even with lengthier warning times. Thinking about the hurricanes that brought death and destruction to this city, one can visualize those disasters in several ways.

One way is to read the destruction as one of Mother Nature having a fit, sending a hurricane into New Orleans and wiping out part of the city. And isn't that a catastrophe? Isn't this an example of our fragility in the face of natural power? But there is another way of looking at it. The Dutch built dikes to keep the ocean back, which is effective because their country, like New Orleans, is mostly underwater. If you go to Holland, they are not underwater, just under the level where water would be if the dikes were not present. The Dutch are very organized people, and their dikes work. So you better be organized if your country or city is supposed to be underwater.

The Dutch have a rule for their dikes: they try to estimate the worst possible oceanic storm that will come in 10,000 years and make sure the dikes will withstand that.

The U.S. Army Corps of Engineers in New Orleans built their "levees" (similar to dikes) for a storm every 100 years. Maybe, that's not so good. Perhaps that is not the wisest of planning because some of New Orleans would normally be underwater and experience flooding from the hurricane. And worse, the state of Louisiana is well known for its political corruption. We could say with some reasonable guesswork that much of the time and resources that could have and should have and planned to go towards fixing the levees didn't. So, along comes a hurricane and people will say, "Oh gosh, wasn't it such a terrible natural disaster?" What makes us so sure that it was a natural disaster? If the infrastructure had been built and maintained properly to the Engineering technical specifications, it would have been much less expensive to do this rather than suffer the consequences of a hurricane's landfall. Is this a natural disaster?

The Guard NCO told me there is a moral lesson here, which is what we think a lot about in the Guard. A natural disaster teaches us lessons that hurricanes and all the flooding (that kills people and destroys property) are predictable. So pointing out that there were steps that could have been taken is the right thing to do. There was an absolute failure of our political, technical, and societal structure – and failure at the human level – because of the corruption to address the problem that everyone knew was there.

The Guard will respond anyway because that is what we do. We know that New Orleans is not prepared, nor will it be ready physically or morally, to withstand another hurricane, at least in the near future.

More than two decades later, after my talk with that Guard NCO, Hurricane Katrina would make landfall in August of 2005. It would become the most damaging and intense hurricane to land in southern Louisiana's history. It caused severe flooding in 80% of New Orleans, with six significant breaches of the city's levees. The collapse of the levee system was termed "the worse engineering catastrophe in U.S. history," made worse by corruption and cronyism in the city's government.

"Cowards die many times before their actual deaths." – Julius Caesar

★ RULE 11

Be Brave; cowards die a thousand times. Face those things you fear most, and only through daring deeds can you be genuinely human.

Theodore Roosevelt was a great military and political leader, statesman, and historian. Although he didn't say it, I'm sure Roosevelt would agree with William Shakespeare's words that cowards die a thousand times before their final death. Roosevelt was a real man – a man's man – much unlike many of today's pretentious, pompous, political sissy men. He was undeniably "the man in the arena," someone who won great acclaim for his fulfillment of personal duty and accountability. Much of that came in positioning the United States for world leadership.

If Roosevelt had read Shakespeare, he would have read the historical-tragic play "Julius Caesar" (1599). Roosevelt would have said it is not the brave man who does not fear. As a Soldier in the Spanish-American War (1898) and as part of the Rough Riders, Colonel Roosevelt would have said that a brave man is trained to fight regardless of his fear. Bravery is not the absence of fear but the willingness to act in the face of it.

Conversely, a coward succumbs to the everyday pressures of life through procrastination and hesitancy. Every day, the coward loses a battle to fear and anxiety, so the coward dies a thousand deaths before the final one. The coward has not sought a meaningful life because cowards never step into the arena to play. The person on the sidelines who jeers players on the field is the epitome of the coward; unwilling to play the game, unable to withstand the challenges and the pressure, incapacitated by spite, envy, and jealousy, they contribute little. Humans are made to carry a load, to push the rock uphill, and to do so without complaint. The coward whines in safety while the hero carries the load and faces danger.

As humans, we innately know that fear is not a trait you want to have to grab you. Even as young children, we know this. In childhood, if one of our friends was frightened of something (or anything), we would joke that our friend was a "chicken" – chickens run from danger. We would taunt that boy (or girl) by chanting "chicken, chicken, chicken" to force bravery or an admission to us that our friend was fearful and unworthy of being part of our friendship circle. It was a hard experience, but we learned early that cowardice does not pay.

The coward's fear is everything. During the Coronavirus pandemic, many people figuratively died a thousand deaths from their fear. They failed to live their lives to the fullest, ran away from large cities toward rural areas, and lied about their health to put themselves ahead of the line for the new vaccine. Those same sorry cowardly souls belittled small towns just months before the pandemic and continue to do so today. Put these men and women in a similar situation today or tomorrow, and their behavior will be unchanged. They are cowards and yet do not realize it.

Today, we can see those fearful folks and what they are. They know we know that their fear is all-consuming. They are cowards who die a thousand times. Cowards know who they are. Be brave.

"Speak softly and carry a big stick." – Theodore Roosevelt

★ **RULE 12**

Be Polite, Be Professional, Walk with a Big Stick

Stop being such a nice person! Don't be timid. Put yourself in a position where you deserve the rewards of your efforts. You can be polite, showing respect to others and some deference to their achievements and that they have intrinsic worth but don't let that politeness devolve into infantile behavior, tepidness, or fear. Be professional; know what you want after having thought it through, and don't be a pushover. Stand up for yourself. Walk with a big stick and allow others who are productive to walk with you, for they receive protection in your presence. Find out what you can do that is valuable and educate yourself about it. That is what makes you powerful. And knowing where you're going is a step in that direction.

Set up some aims for yourself, aims that you actually value. Plan a life you would like to have. You will have to put some effort into your life, and you need to be motivated to do that. And, you need to consider your life across several dimensions – if you were taking care of yourself properly, with intimate relationships, friendships, family, career, time outside work, and regulating your use of alcohol and dangerous drugs. Establish for yourself a valued goal (your motivation is derived from this goal) and assemble a set of required tasks that allow you to obtain that goal.

Setting up these aims is how you can be excited about what you have to do when you wake up in the morning. You look forward to the day. Specify your long-term ideal (follow your dream) – and also specify a place you want to stay away from (that terrifies you if you fail) – and those tasks linked to that goal are what motivates you. You do that partly by referring to social norms; such as being polite, respectful, diligent and conscientious, being professional, staying on track, having a balanced life, making the correct life-choice sacrifices, and walking properly with your head up and your shoulders back – walk with a big stick.

I often advise young men and women on how to prepare themselves for those who want to join the U.S. military and also those wishing to obtain an engineering or science degree from a respected university. A greater degree of dedication and considerable motivation is necessary inside institutions. Success calls for a high degree of merit to advance. Excellence is required. These two paths teach those real-world skills that are useful, not just in a career but to become genuinely the person you want to be and be good at what you do and be someone you would respect. You will learn the use of cold logic, respect for the profession and for others, doing your job expertly, the importance of being reliable and trustworthy, having confidence in your ability, possessing a positive attitude, having the capacity to set goals and knowledgeably obtain them, and so on, and the list is lengthy; and as it should be.

Each of those young people was provided a list of things they should do (sacrifices) to make it easier as they transition from civilian to Soldier or University student. They are told to be polite (you can't fake it), be professional (know your stuff), and walk with a big stick (walk with the confidence of someone who knows what they want). The feedback from young men and women has been overwhelmingly positive.

They say that without this advice, they would not have finished their military training or an academic engineering/science degree and, in many cases, excelled beyond their imagination. It was the best time of their lives. They were on the adventure of their lives.

During the early days of the Iraq War, Soldiers of the 1st Cavalry Division made progress on the battlefield by stamping out a growing terror campaign of nasty, brutish insurgents. Their motto was, "Be Polite, Be Professional, Be Prepared to Kill." The motto would say a lot about how the divisions' Soldiers conducted their mission; always polite, strictly professional, and armed with the most modern weaponry ever devised by the mind and hand of humankind. It was a difficult task and yet still a noble cause. Always fighting to win over the disgruntled Iraqi citizens to our side, win their hearts and minds, bring them into the modern world, and reject totalitarianism and the killing and torture of innocents, Christians, gays, and Coalition Soldiers.

There is something that humans greatly value and appreciate more than just about anything else, and that is respect for the strong and humble warrior. Like President Teddy Roosevelt said, "Speak softly and carry a big stick." That stick he refers to is the power of your words, actions, and your reputation and your team. Without it, you have nothing, and you and those around you will inescapably suffer terribly.

Be polite, be professional, and walk with a big stick.

"There are no secrets to success. It is the result of preparation, hard work, and learning from failure." – Colin Powell

★ **RULE 13**

The Sacrifices you chose to (and must) make

We grew up in the Deep South and attended church services every Wednesday and Sunday with family and neighbors. Like so many boys of that young age, I was fidgety in my seat, squirming because I was bored and impatient. Sitting in the pews next to my brother and sister, our Pastor would re-tell Biblical stories that included making sacrifices to God. It was hard for my brother and me to understand why anyone would give up something of value like that. Connecting the dots was not easy. The young boys thought that was stupid for adults to do, and yet we were wrong.

Those stories of sacrifice were about giving up something in the present so that you can improve the future. Of all things discovered by humans, this is one of our central ideas, a way of seeing ourselves that sets humans apart from animals.

Understanding what sacrifice means and its connection to the future takes a long time and deep thought. On the surface, the idea of sacrifice was presented as rituals of burnt offerings and animal sacrifice. It seemed so archaic and outdated, unnecessary and wasteful to me. In Biblical stories, the sacrificial purpose was to stay on God's good side, much like the original sacrifice in the story Cain and Able. In that story, Cain (Adam and Eve's older son) sacrifices to God, but his gifts are less than adequate. This "unfairness" (in the thinking of Cain) frustrates Cain, and his bitterness and resentfulness revealed itself when he ultimately kills his brother Able. This story tells us much about the idea of thinking about the future and what happens if we fail to do so.

Brother Terry (my sister remembers calling our pastor by this name) of the Mer Rouge Southern Baptist church taught us that if we look at these texts, we just might understand that the ancients were trying to understand their own existence and explain the means to be fruitful and multiply (i.e., successful). He said that to be a good person, you must sacrifice properly. He told us that you get to choose the sacrifice, but you do not get an option not to sacrifice. And, a sacrifice must be of something genuinely valuable; else, it will be unworthy, and in the end, we will be bitter and resentful when it fails to gain us what we desire.

One of the more interesting thoughts about the Bible's Old Testament and the story of Moses and the slavery of his people in Egypt is that they rejected the path of Cain. Every time God strikes at the Egyptian Pharaoh and at their Jewish slaves, which is often, Moses says that it is the Jews themselves who must have done something wrong. Moses proclaims the Jews must set themselves straight. That is an unbelievably courageous outlook. It is courageous because this thinking is an advantageous alternative to blaming others for their wrongs and failures, blaming their many unseen gods, or chalking it up to fate. You take that responsibility upon yourself and, in the case of Moses, lead his people to the Promised Land.

This idea is no trivial matter.

We, as humans, can imagine a future, and that is how we differ fundamentally from all others in the animal kingdom. We can see ourselves in the future and look at how we can fail (and be miserable) and how we can be successful (with a life of satisfaction). If you can reject the misery and look at yourself to sacrifice properly, you can move forward into that future.

The most difficult question is, "What are you aiming at?" You are trying to improve the future as a consequence of your efforts today. That is what those Biblical and ancient stories tell us, which is why the stories are of such great importance. Ultimately, this is about knowing how to represent yourself – the good you – in the world and be who you might be. Don't be Cain.

I learned to sacrifice certain things that provided value in pursuing a military career and making myself a better person and successful family man (being more than I could be). This is the same idea discussed among those who desire a career; that you get out of it what you put into it. All merit-based organizations demand hard work, integrity, loyalty, and selfless service. But this effort is highly demanding on one's time and energy.

Below are sacrifices we can make to increase our chances of a more prosperous future:

1. **Friends who are lazy, fatalistic, or who themselves have no plans in life other than partying, playing games, and having fun.** *It was not easy, but we told them we could no longer be part of our lives. They are dragging us down, and that has to stop. Their aim is down. Our aim is up.*
2. **Television and movies.** *Wasting many hours each week on entertainment serves little purpose. Watching people on a screen do exciting things does not help. Gain back those hours and use them for your family, friends, and job/career/study.*
3. **Social media.** *Like alcohol and drugs, social media can be highly addicting. It takes up many hours that could be better put to good use.*
4. **Shiny Objects.** *There are very few things we need to live properly. A house or apartment, maybe a car, adequate food and*

water, and clothing. Other than that, we have little need for fancy trucks, boats, toys, and jewelry; we 'want' them because those shiny objects are fun, and others have them too. Learn to live a simpler life without them.

5. **Instant Gratification.** *Learn to live within your means, don't go into debt, avoid fancy and expensive clothes, resist fads and fashion, and learn to say 'no' to what you don't need.*

Making the proper sacrifices takes intense discipline and is challenging. It requires focus. It requires delayed gratification. By proper sacrifice, you don't have to spend time figuring out the latest fashion trends or fads or what makes you look better. Discipline and focus are admirable traits associated with success and a good life.

Choose your sacrifices; don't let life choose them for you.

"Never give in, never give in, never; never; never; never-in nothing, great or small, large or petty – never give in except to convictions of honour and good sense." – Winston Churchill

★ **RULE 14**

Never surrender your sword. Never give up. Never despair. Fight for everything you are, and you will discover that which you thought was impossible.

If you fall behind, run faster.

In days of the past, surrendering a Soldier's sword symbolized the admission of defeat or arrest. Often the military victor would break the sword in half and return it broken to the defeated to symbolize the humiliation of defeat.

We are often too quick to "surrender our swords" when engaged in the field of ideas or in achieving a better life for ourselves and our families. We give up for various reasons, mainly because we believe there is little to gain from a fight or fear the consequences of losing our job or some object of affection. Modern men and women see themselves as small and ineffective, too small to make a difference, or too timid to stand up and be seen. If you see yourself as small and ineffective, you have admitted defeat, and you are correct.

Some individuals are rocks in the stream. Water flows past the rock without affecting it in its place. Strong leaders are like the rock and refuse to allow themselves to be swept away by the trivialities of the day. Strong men and women may fear the unknown but will not run away like cowards. We have great affection for those willing to stand and hold their ground.

The hero is that person who, with little power and with plenty of faults and frailties, nevertheless slays the Dragon and captures the gold or princess as well. We read about the sword-wielding dragon slayer of legend from the Ancient world captured in the story of the Archangel Michael or St. George.

Our ancient ancestors had a preoccupation with fire-breathing Dragons. And in classical Greek mythology, the story elements of the Dragon being slain by a hero with a sword originates. Apollo, Cadmus, Perseus, and Heracles were just a few that tipped our interest in the grand meta-stories for hundreds of years.

We are fascinated with the sword (an offensive weapon) and the philosophy of never surrendering your sword. The sword symbolizes strength, duty, and honor in Western society. "Fight to the death" was a common refrain among military foot soldiers and sailors of old. To run from a fight was more than cowardice; it was an insult to your brethren, betrayal of the worse kind, shame to your family, and an unspeakable dishonor to your state.

Never surrender your sword. Never give up. Fight!

"Nothing can stop the man with the right mental attitude from achieving his goal; nothing on earth can help the man with the wrong mental attitude." — Thomas Jefferson

★ RULE 15

Develop a thick skin. Be mentally tough. Two essential traits in life are a spine and a sense of humor. Arm yourself with humor, and thrive with camaraderie. You are the leader of your life.

Often, I tell the story about my first duty assignment in the Army. Two new arrivals were paired up and sent to a small military base in West Germany, located just outside a rural town - Siegelsbach. The base was tiny but important. It housed nuclear weapons. Those assigned had a tough, tedious job and failure to secure the "nukes" was unacceptable (we would not want a nuclear warhead to go missing). The Soldiers were rough, and their morale was constantly under assault because their job was one of the least desirable; tedious, uninspiring, far away from civilization or the nearest town, where alcohol was plentiful, and little to do outside work.

Upon arrival, Jerome and I were given nicknames. Mine was "Satt" — an easy choice since it was short for Satterfield. Jerome was given the nickname "Dipstick" because he was a mechanic, and his uniform was stained. The problem was that Jerome wasn't too happy about the nickname. That was a mistake. He should have taken it with a smile and good humor. In addition, "Dipstick" was irritable and a complainer; he whined in one of those high, irritating voices when given a task. Soon after our arrival, Soldiers in our unit began pulling tricks on Jerome. One joke was to put a condom in his web gear and then publically call attention to it. Jerome reacted poorly; he couldn't take the joke. Everyone got a good laugh, which made him more irritable and miserable.

The Soldiers were testing him. Jerome, can you take a joke? Can you take a bit of dirty humor? Can you at least be a little fun yourself? Soldiers wanted to know if Jerome could pass the test to be part of their team and be helpful. Could he take it and dish it out too? A month later, Jerome was sent to our Brigade's headquarters, never to return. These Soldiers had tested him to see if he could take the pressure. They might need to depend upon him if the base was ever attacked by a terrorist (which was a real threat in the name of the Red Brigade). You don't want someone in your military unit who cannot take the stress or who cannot be relied upon.

I had several nicknames in the Army. Most were okay. A few were dirty but funny (so I won't repeat them here). But there is a camaraderie around those nicknames. There is also a test surrounding them to see what you're made of. Are you a wimp? Can you handle the purposeful irritation and return it in kind? If you can, you can be part of the group. Maybe we can rely on you. The issue was not that Jerome could take some random joking insults, but he could not laugh at himself. If Dipstick had just laughed off the nickname and taken it as a badge of honor, that would have been the end of it. All he had to do was take some ribbing with good grace, refuse to suck up to the officers, and do his job and not have others do it for him. Every person must be tested before they can be trusted.

Guarding nuclear weapons is mind-numbing, occasionally dangerous, and always difficult. What made these jobs tolerable was the tremendous amount of camaraderie surrounding them. Working up in the military ranks, the same level of camaraderie faded. It's thrilling to be part of a team doing dangerous and tough work and simultaneously have a cruel yet outrageously entertaining time while you are doing it.

You can develop a thick skin around these nicknames and the dirty tricks played on you. You can tell others about them and laugh a little with the jokesters. If you do, the jokes won't get too vicious and mean because they don't have to. Can we poke fun at you? Yes, please do. By doing so, by being part of the joke and not the butt of the joke, others will help you keep your feet on the ground. Arm yourself with a sense of humor. That's a good thing to arm yourself with.

Can you develop a thick skin? Yes, we all can. Do you need extensive, broad-based experiences to have a thick skin? It helps, but no, you don't. The solution is to be humble and optimistic; have a sense of humor, and look people in the eye and smile. That is the way to deal with failure, rejection, and insults that come your way. You can face it. Stand up, hold your shoulders back, speak the truth, and reject resentment and bitterness. Your decisions in life will always be questioned, second-guessed, insulted, and often on a grand scale. Act with grace and humility. Never lose sight of the fact that there is a downside to reacting badly and that if you can overcome your arrogance, you will be more likable. You will have a thick skin and possess more enjoyment in your life.

"It takes courage to grow up and become who you really are." –
e. e. cummings

★ **RULE 16**

**Stop acting like a 10-Year-Old. Grow up and go on an
adventure. Take on some responsibility. You are
answerable to your own destiny.**

A mature adult is the person with the instinctive desire to
adopt responsibility for one's self and others and do so
willingly. That person is the one interested in the unknown,
has the yearning to explore, find new things, carry a heavy
load, and be a rebel in a world of safety and conformity.
Mature adulthood is based on the universal and ancient need
to be accountable for one's actions. This mission is the
ancient call to adventure and heroism.

True enough, the burden is not and will never be easy. So
stop acting like a 10-year-old and get on with it.

An old story makes this point from Greek mythology about
the Titan god Atlas. In this famous story told worldwide,
Atlas carries the world's weight on his shoulders. Atlas is a
universal symbol of endurance, strength, and resoluteness, as
he calmly bears his pain of responsibility. To this day, Atlas
remains one of the most enduring themes in art and literature.
Why is this story so alluring? Why is it that we are
sympathetic to Atlas? Why do we admire him so? The
answer is that we are instinctively drawn to those who can

hold the world (or family, community, team) together and voluntarily bear the weight of its problems.

Choose the weight you have to carry. Choose it so that you can justify your existence to yourself and end your day and think, "Look, I did what I needed to do to set things right today." And now, you don't have to feel the shame of your failures. And, as you carry that weight, it will gain you a bit of self-respect, which will carry you through terrible times. Carrying that heavy load gives your life meaning and keeps despair and depression away.

Do those things that make you better, and hold onto the humility necessary to do so. Take on those lowly tasks that need doing, and do them with a smile on your face and contentment in your heart. Some of your fondest memories will be from those times, your camaraderie with others doing those tasks, and you will look back upon them with a smile and a longing that you may say, "I miss those times." The "why" is that you carried the responsibility and did so willingly, contently, and thankfully, not with an arrogant attitude. If you are unhappy, look around and see if there are opportunities, even flawed ones, you can take on. You can exploit those imperfect prospects to learn and grow.

Stop acting like a 10-year-old. You are answerable to your own destiny.

"Never let the fear of striking out keep you from playing the game."
— Babe Ruth

★ **RULE 17**

It's your turn in the "box." Be accountable for your actions. Get off your butt, play the game, and move on with your life.

Decision time. Either you choose to be fully accountability for your decisions and actions in life, or you don't. There are no maybe, kinda, or half-measures; this is an all-or-nothing performance. Life is about having a family, friends, a job (or school), plans for time outside work, and good physical and mental health. You should possess most of these, but if you don't have any, you don't have much. Choose a proper goal in your life, get something noble to aim at and orient yourself toward it. If you adopt responsibility for your life, you have made a conscious decision and are admitting to the world that it's your time in the "box."

Electrical lineman Johnny McGrath, Jr. had 15 years of experience with Pennsylvania Power and Light (PP&L). He would say, "If you don't make this [electrical] connection correctly, you die." And, he says with all seriousness, "A greater tragedy is that you will also kill your buddy." We sent four of our linemen to PP&L Lineman School for additional training on medium-voltage electrical distribution systems, one of the most dangerous jobs in the world (and one of the better paid). McGrath was so focused, one of our men said, he could cut steel with his intensity. If you wanted to be a lineman, you had to understand that you were fully accountable for what did or did not happen in the "box.' Know what needs doing, and do it. There are no half-measures. Safety is all or nothing. Failure is death. Yes, indeed, men like McGrath are rare. They know that to play the game of life, you have to be on top of everything; dedicated, responsible, technically proficient, intolerant of stupidity or laziness, and hard working.

Adoption of responsibility means having clear, measurable life goals, and while those goals may change (our preferences can morph over time), we should embrace the real-world fact we might fail. There is real fear in adopting this strategy. It means knowing the conditions of failure, like losing your job or family or money or failing in school. It explains why so many resist specifying their goals. We don't like to clarify conditions for failure because it is so painful. Sometimes we think it better to remain willfully ignorant and infant-like. The problem is, in that case, we will fail all the time; we just won't know it until we fail so badly that our life is over. That can quickly occur by age 30 or 40. Imagine a 30-year-old infant, and their life is over.

The question is, "How can you be productive and live a good life?" The right way is to be specific about what you want and set up those things you need to do to get what you want. Perhaps you will not hit these things – these intermediate goals – all the time. Maybe you hit them only 50% of the time. That's okay because you will get better over time, and maybe you can achieve 51% tomorrow or next week. Do not be consumed by falling short of your goals. Keep at it. People with goals succeed because they know where they're going. If you don't have an aim, you will get there 0% of the time. If you're alive and genuinely want to be an upright, valuable person to yourself, your family, and your community, grasp responsibility and be content that it's your time in the "box."

Be accountable for what you do. Get off your butt, play the game, and move on with your life. You don't have to be like lineman McGrath, but he is the kind of man you can look up to and learn his way to a successful life.

It's your turn in the "box." Be accountable for all that you do.

"Only those who dare to fail greatly can ever achieve greatly." –
Robert F. Kennedy

★ **RULE 18**

**Embrace failure, learn and move on. Remember that failure
is only temporary.**

Failure has been around since Adam and Eve ate the apple in the
Garden of Eden. They would "become like God" if they ate it,
so claimed the serpent. Adam and Eve believed the lie and chose
to eat the apple in disobedience to God, which began "the Fall of
Man." Of course, it did not take long for Adam and Eve to
discover that eating the forbidden fruit was a grave mistake and
that they were responsible (although Adam initially denied his
actions and blamed it on Eve).

Failure does not always stare us in the face, and even when it
does, we often turn away and ignore it. The most significant
failures of humankind occurred during the 20th Century;
although we had the opportunity, we didn't stop them.
Preventing Adolf Hitler's rise to power and the Jewish Holocaust
he perpetuated. Stopping Mao's "Great Leap Forward" and the
subsequent great Chinese famine. Thwarting the Imperial
Japanese Army's "rape of Nanking" and other Chinese cities.
And, of course, the great Holodomor, the Soviet Union's human-

engineered famine in the country of Ukraine. And Cambodia's killing fields. The list goes on.

The most common reason people fail is they have never set the criteria for success. They drift toward some undefined goal, and when their life does not work out, they crash and burn, blaming others or fate. It is only natural that we want to avoid failure, even in the smallest of things. Failure can bring embarrassment, resentment, and frustration. However, the fact is that no great success was ever achieved without failure. It may have been one or a series of failures, but failure is a necessary stepping stone to achieving our dreams.

My experience is that you can have something if you really want it. If you want it and are willing to reorient your life to make the probability that your desire will happen, it will occur. Of course, you must sacrifice something worthwhile to achieve your goal. That is the sacrificial idea that you cannot get everything you desire, and everything will have a cost.

Failing to try, giving up, or standing on the sidelines watching others in the "box" are real failures because there is no willingness or motivation to make the required sacrifice. If you want to be a medical doctor or highly respected professional, there is a lengthy, difficult, expensive road ahead through higher education and apprentice training. Not everyone is willing to make that sacrifice, nor are some even capable. What is the point in life if you don't at least try to achieve something you believe is important?

The symbolism of the forbidden fruit demonstrates the idea that humans have aims and the free will to move toward them. But they must have the desire and the will to make the proper sacrifice.

Failure is the inevitable first step. Embrace failure, learn and move on.

"Some people are inherently likable. If you're not — work on it. It may even improve your social life." — Antonin Scalia

★ **RULE 19**

Be likable, reject seeking popularity.

On our trip to Washington, D.C., a group of senior military officers (of which I was a member) were given a tour of the Rayburn House Office Building (it houses the U.S. House of Representatives). This place is where to go if you want to find your Congressional representative. Fortunately, it was not crowded that day, and we were lucky to meet several Congress members in their offices. We discovered that each elected member we spoke to was exceptionally likable. It did not matter their political party, where they were from, young or old, or what they were doing. Each made us feel welcome and that we were important. The lesson would seem to be that being likable helps get you elected.

Psychologists are consistent about having a likable disposition. By age 4, more likable children are generally more successful later in life with their jobs, family, friends, and other measures of well-being. When adults teach children to be likable, other children and adults will want to be around them, play games, read to them, and offer help.

In adulthood, being likable opens doors to greater opportunities. I witnessed many times when senior military commanders (who possessed information that would benefit all Soldiers) selectively dispensed the information. They gave it to those they liked most. Whether this was an unconscious act or not, it matters little; likable Soldiers were getting more chances to advance themselves through more opportunities. It should come as no surprise that the higher-ranked Soldiers are also more likable. They also receive more military awards than those with less likable temperaments. Was it fair? Probably not, but the answer is irrelevant because that is the way of the world.

Of course, it is only human to be attracted to people who have a pleasant disposition, are genuine, less likely to judge you, are more honest, smile more often, and are open about their thinking and their own life. Likable people are viewed as more loyal, brave, dependable, cheerful, and caring. These are valuable traits in any walk of life.

On the other hand, be aware of the allure of popularity. We all want to "fit in," and deep down, we might even want to be popular. Many seek popularity by manipulation and pandering to gain status. We've seen them before – the kid that has outlandishly huge parties when his parents are away, the class clown who wants to be the center of attention or the person who controls relationships to gain popularity. They will do anything to be noticed, accepted, or approved of. Unfortunately, these status seekers can become anxious and depressed and sometimes develop addiction problems. Status-seeking efforts are far easier to achieve than putting in the effort to be likable. Don't be fooled; popularity does not bring respect or true and lasting friendship.

Be likable, reject seeking popularity.

"He whose life has a why can bear almost any how."
– Friedrich Nietzsche

★ **RULE 20**

Treat yourself well. Treat yourself as if you were in charge of another person. Keep the promises you make to yourself.

The fact is, we don't treat ourselves well. Interestingly, people are more likely to dispense doctor-prescribed medication to their pets than themselves. We have a moral obligation to care for ourselves because our being requires us to serve selflessly, and we can only do so when we are well enough and strong enough to take on the day. Take care of yourself as if you have value and that there is meaning in your existence. Taking care of yourself means getting healthier (physically and mentally), expanding your knowledge, pursuing the goals you want, and speaking about and following your values.

Fail to care for yourself, and you will burden others more, perhaps magnifying their own difficulties and challenges. Whatever you are, whatever you believe you are, the truth is that you are part of a vast, complex human network. The average person during their lifetime will know about a thousand people. And each of them knows about a thousand people. That circumstance puts us one person away from a million people and two away from a billion people. Your worth is greater than you might think.

Regardless of our own inadequacies and problems, there remains intrinsic worth in each of us. As a consequence of this ancient and fundamentally Western idea (a Judeo-Christian belief), people have intrinsic worth, which is why we are duty-bound to treat ourselves properly. And if we do so correctly, our lives will become more meaningful. By caring for ourselves, we can become more educated and wiser, and we become a model for other people, a better father, or sister, and we are less ridden by that gnawing shame that undermines all of us and says that we are not who we should be.

Philosophically each person has an essential worth that we must recognize. How else to be part of the good social order and achieve personal, familial, and communal success than believing in yourself and having the guts to take ownership of yourself? Reject self-recrimination. Whatever you are, you are not a lone spirit. Even if you think you are alone, the reality is here to push you into acknowledging that you are connected to others.

While we are all subject to bad breaks and the random unfairness of life, this does not give us a license to live by the whims of our barbaric wants and desires. Floating through life and deteriorating from all the self-indulgent, adolescent-like, narcissistic behavior is a recipe for disaster. This arrogant approach may gain you a bit of instant gratification, but we must realize that there is no substitute for taking small steps to serve others selflessly. Forgive yourself for your mistakes, recognize that you are not worthless, and although you might just be lazy, you are not useless. You will slip up sometimes. But, you will slowly gain the confidence you need to take on new things in life if you do. Give yourself a chance and see how much better you can be.

Treat yourself as if you were in charge of another person. Keep promises you make to yourself.

OUTTAKE: The best cup of coffee ever!

Learning to be a reliable, ethical, and loyal person can be difficult. The time with others, training, studying, and working helps that process. In 1983, I was a brand new U.S. Army Second Lieutenant attending the Infantry Officer Basic Course. At the end of a particularly grueling three-week training phase of the mechanized infantry course, we stopped long enough to have the first cup of coffee in as many weeks.

We had learned that being a good Soldier is fraught with obstacles; going without coffee was an unexpected, difficult problem that surprised us all. "Anyone can go without coffee," we thought. Many of us laughed and said we could do anything for three weeks, "It's just time anyway from the barracks, and our trainers will know we can take it." Little did we understand that we would get dull headaches (a chemical withdrawal from the caffeine drug). With daily temperature highs in the upper 90s and humidity hovering around 100%, our headaches were magnified many times.

In that field training, we learned the advantages of having some technical knowledge, the advantage of positive and creative thinking, physical resilience, and intelligence. More than anything else, we learned to appreciate the fact that to lead others – as we would do later during combat – a military officer must inspire, motivate, and lead through example.

> *"The challenge of leadership is to be strong, but not rude; be kind, but not weak; be bold, but not bully; be thoughtful, but not lazy; be humble, but not timid; be proud, but not arrogant; have humor, but without folly." – Jim Rohn, entrepreneur, author, and motivational speaker*

The most important thing for military officers is never to lose the ability to inspire others so that others can be great in whatever they do. A leader who does not inspire will not be a leader for long. We had this drummed into our heads every day. At the end of each day, as we prepared to sleep (with 50% security provided by our fellow officers), we discussed that day's lessons.

On day 21 of mechanized training, I was sitting next to an old M113A2 Armored Personnel Carrier, thinking what tomorrow would bring, when another lieutenant – Jack – brought me a cup of hot coffee. Where did he get this great cup of coffee? My friend had mixed water, instant coffee, non-dairy creamer, and raw sugar from our C-rations and heated it by burning C-4 explosive. This coffee is the kind you throw into the ground; it would taste so awful. Yet, at the time, it was the best cup of coffee I ever had and have ever had since. I thought at the time how lucky I was. Our mood immediately improved. A smile came across our faces. It certainly didn't hurt that Jack and I were drinking our first cup of coffee and the other Lieutenants were envious. We were grateful despite the suffering we endured during training; the coffee made it better.

I'm sure today, if I had that cup of coffee, I would spit it out. But at the time, it was the best coffee anyone could have given me. Jack was trying to say thanks for my encouraging him during the training. Teamwork works! And to this day, I remember that coffee, with some dust, a few small twigs, and two ants swirling around in the cup, and yet it is forever my best Cup of Joe … ever!

Be humble. Don't take anything for granted. At a moment's notice, your world can change and not for the better. Be prepared to be the first to stand up with courage and vigilance. You will someday be the only person ready to save the day. And remember that even a cup of coffee can make a difference.

"There are three kinds of men. The one that learns by reading. The few who learn by observation. The rest of them have to pee on the electric fence for themselves." – Will Rogers

★ **RULE 21**

Learn to write properly, speak plainly, and read well. Writing is formalized thinking.

Practice your words. To speak is the most powerful thing about you.

The purpose of a proper childhood upbringing is to teach us to think. Thinking makes us act correctly. Thinking helps us win the battles of our lives. If you can read and write and speak, you are a thinker and cannot be defeated. Nothing can keep you from success. The idea that proper thinking can rescue us from the depths of failure is no theory; it is the basis of human existence.

That is why good writing is so important. To write is the most powerful weapon you can possibly have in your rucksack of personal tools. Suppose you can write well, make a presentation, lay out a proposal and a logical argument, and formulate your arguments coherently. In that case, people will give you money and opportunities beyond your dreams. You will gain influence and capabilities more incredible than your imagination. What you do has value, and others will reward you for it.

You learn to think best by writing and speaking. The best thing a person can do is read and write and do it every day, at least a couple of hours of practice daily, even when your writing is poorly constructed and your reading is slow and difficult. Read and write about things you believe are necessary or of interest or funny. See if you can discover those things you believe to be true. Practice builds a foundation, and reading and writing are unbelievably helpful in pushing you to understand better and formulate ideas. If you look at highly successful folks, there are several reasons they are winners. One reason is that they are especially good at speaking about what they aim at and strategizing, negotiating, and enticing people with a vision forward.

What is of the utmost importance is that our thinking is free so that we can visualize all outcome possibilities (even if we poorly do so) and look into the future to see what could be the best possible outcomes for the good of ourselves and others. All successful societies are built upon the idea that cultural adaptation (and its avoidance of corruption) requires the free thought of its citizens. In addition, if we are motivated by others listening to what we have to say and if what we say is good, honest, forthright, and valuable, then others will let us know they appreciate our way of thinking.

Teaching people to speak gives them the power to control their lives, which is highly motivating. It is a mystery why this is not taught to children and young adults. Our formal education system is set up to do precisely that: to teach us to freely think, speak, write, and read. The freedom to speak, even if poorly practiced or offensive, is necessary for any advancement of any advanced culture. This is the free speech argument. It's the foundation of Western civilization.

Millennia ago, it was the strongest man who had his way. Brute strength mattered most; violence was the way of the world, and the physically weak were quick to die or be enslaved. Language slowly developed, and while its purpose had many uses, one primary one was to substitute for violence. We could now work out our conflicts verbally. While what we say can be challenging to hear and frustrating, it is better than direct violence against us. Those that are physically the strongest no longer rule; it is those who are the most persuasive, inspiring, trustworthy, receptive to ideas, and humble.

Consequently, get your words together for honest communication. That makes you irresistible. If you can communicate directly and honestly, you are unstoppable. Learn to find your authentic voice. Every time you deviate from an honest conversation you are having through lies and deceit, you corrupt yourself and so avoid it. When you can formulate your arguments, it becomes a part of how you view the world. It guides your future actions. Work to become as articulate and clear as possible. Doing so is difficult and takes practice, but nothing is more practical and noble.

Someone once said, "Reading good books is like a conversation with the finest minds of the past." If you can read well, and you practice reading daily and put forward the proper motivation in yourself to understand as much as you can, then you can be and do whatever you wish. Those who succeed never avoid reading; it is where the spark for innovation and greatness lies. You already know how to be ordinary in ordinary times. Be extraordinary; read as if your life depended upon it. It does.

If you learn to read well, write properly, and speak plainly, you are headed for success in whatever you decide to do.

"Loyalty is a big part of football, and it shows if you are a real man or not." – Jack Wilshere

★ **RULE 22**

Be loyal to your family, respect them, honor and protect them. Dedicate yourself to their well-being, for they are the ones who are on your team.

Loyalty is too frequently underrated and underappreciated. We are all flawed beings with curious tastes and attractions. We also tend to veer off the path of good to follow our own desires, often searching for something we frequently cannot identify. While searching to make our life meaningful, we must never forget that our families are supporters of our welfare. There are tragedies we will inevitably know – our parents die, our best friends move away, and our spouse leaves us without a goodbye. It matters not whether they deserve our loyalty, and perhaps they deserve nothing or worse. Yet, with loyalty to our family, we send a clear message and announcement to those around us that family is essential and has great value.

I've always believed that family (and friends) is more than the immediate practical value of distributing household duties, sharing costs, and working together on daily tasks. Families teach us valuable lessons, encourage us, warn us of impending danger, and demonstrate how to be a better person.

Unfortunately, there is an idea in the West that the family structures of the past are unnecessary or impractical. Some will tell us that the traditional nuclear family is somehow unworthy of our allegiance, a patriarchal structure, and that it can be unfair and demeaning. I disagree. This failure to accept the family is tipping our moral scales in the wrong direction. Rejection of the father and mother leads to a sea of young men and women adrift of values and honor. Crime increases, cities burn, self-value declines, and suicide soars. Our family is the refuge of a good man and a good woman.

It was not that long ago that we looked into the role families play in the success of Soldiers. No formal studies exist that address how families influence military success. Most research is restricted to how the military lifestyle affects the family. Our interest was the reverse; how the family affects the military. The team investigating discovered that those raised in stable, two-parent families make up the hardest working, most dedicated, most trustworthy, and resilient military members. If you want something done, give it to the best Soldier in your unit; that person is likely from a stable family. We also discovered, on average, that married military members with children make the best Soldiers.

The impact of family on military success is at least anecdotally evident to those who spent any length of time in our military services. When making an effective Soldier, the family is the best predictor. Loyalty to the family (and friends and community) is the precursor to great soldiering and great families.

It is up to each of us to stand up for the family. The family's role in raising the child harks back to when humans first walked the earth. No one can argue with any legitimacy that families are failing us or that the family does not deserve our loyalty. Doing so will spell disaster for the youngest.

Be loyal to your family.

"Surround yourself with good people. People who are going to be honest with you and look out for your best interests." – Derek Jeter

★ **RULE 23**

Surround yourself with good people who want the best for you; learn from those who are better, faster, and wiser than you are; avoid 'negative nellies.'

In the study of history, we learn that some of the greatest leaders had something in common. They surrounded themselves with good people. Alexander the Great, also known as King of Macedon (from 336-323 B.C.), discovered this value as a child. Alexander would improve his combat skills as a boy by fighting only young men significantly stronger and faster than him. It is widely known that the best way to improve a set of skills is to practice with someone better than you. You must work harder, think faster, and learn the fundamentals. You will sweat more, have sore muscles, and experience frustration and disappointment, but your skills will improve after gaining a better know-how. Folks who are better than you will push you to your limit and beyond what you think is possible.

The idea of practicing (or competing) with someone better than you extends to your education and career success and why it is so important to surround yourself with people who are winners.

U.S. combat leaders today use this idea to improve the proficiency of their fighting forces. Beginning in the early part of World War II, the U.S. Army and Marines brought in highly-skilled civilian experts in Martial Arts to teach their men how to fight effectively hand-to-hand. This program was so successful that it continued after the war and is used today. Combat leaders understood that you had to be ready, disciplined, skilled, and dogged in the fight to beat an enemy.

There is no substitute for hard work and the right attitude – a firm willingness – to learn from those who are better than you. This is why it is critical to surround yourself with good people, the right people who genuinely care about you and who will make you better, better than you believe you could ever be.

There will always be obstacles and naysayers on our road to success. These can be family, friends, schoolmates, colleagues, teachers, coaches, or anyone from any walk of life. It is rarely a stranger. These 'nervous nellies' are the people who live a life of disappointment and turmoil, usually of their choosing. Unfortunately, they seem never to manage to elevate themselves and never accept their place in life without blaming others. Worse, they will try to bring you down right along with them. Avoid these people if at all possible. You may feel good trying to save this person; your intent is moral, but your effort will be wasted, and you may destroy yourself. You are not obligated to associate with those making your life worse. Move away from people like that.

Surround yourself with good people who want the best for you.

"Blessed are the meek, for they shall inherit the earth." —
Matthew 5:5, the Bible

★ **RULE 24**

Share your foxhole with someone who can fight like the devil.

I learned an important lesson from a Doughboy who fought on the battlefields of World War I (the "War to End All Wars"). One day, he came over to say hello. The new neighbor, Mr. Jed Neidigh, had a big smile, a head full of white hair, and a firm grip. "Howdy!" he said as he welcomed us. We were new arrivals in the neighborhood. "I see you're an Army man, just like me." Mr. Neidigh was the Doughboy next door for the next eight years as we lived in State College, Pennsylvania.

The guns of the First World War had fallen eerily silent in 1918. Seven decades after the Armistice signing, I met a man who fought in that war; businessman, family man, and now the Doughboy who lived next door. He had been part of the Great War. His advice was simple; to be a better man, share your foxhole with someone who can fight like the devil.

Doughboy Neidigh told the story of how the Allied forces were taking a terrible beating from the Germans during the Third Battle of the Aisne in 1918. It was brutal combat, which you cannot know or "feel" unless you've been there. He said he lost his rifle one day in one of many attacks. Never, ever, lose your rifle, for it protects you and your buddies. But, he told me, "since there were thousands [of rifles] just lying around, I just picked one up." The implication was obvious. He cried when he talked about his unit's massive casualties from large-caliber artillery shelling. After the shelling, the fighting was often hand-to-hand, with the bayonet or trench knife or brass knuckles or the ax. A buddy who could fight "like the devil" kept you alive.

Deep down in my soul, it was difficult to understand how the foot soldiers of WWI could conduct a mass attack across a vast, open no-man's land in the face of a well-equipped, determined, and experienced enemy. Those large Infantry charges resulted in horrific casualties in the tens of thousands in just minutes. It is impossible today to grasp the immenseness of such a battle.

It took strong men, men that would scare you, to look at them, to fight those battles. Fighting the Hun (the German) required mental and physical strength, which is uncommon in the West. In this war, you died if you were with a unit of weak men. If you were lucky enough to be with the strong, with those that could use the bayonet and not even blink an eye, those Doughboys that fought like the devil, then and only then would you survive to fight another battle. Today, having someone on your side who knows how to get the job done, call out the weaklings, and fight the bad guys, makes you one of the lucky ones.

There is a phrase from the Bible that is applicable here but often misinterpreted. It is written that "Blessed are the meek, for they shall inherit the earth." The word meek does not mean weak, feeble, or fragile in its most literal sense but refers to someone who has the skill of using force and then decides when to use that strength to protect others. Biblical researchers say it means something like a strong guardian walking with a sword sheathed in a scabbard, ready to use it at a moment's notice. Scholars agree that this is a closer meaning of the text, and when meek is read as "strength," it makes more sense in context. Brute strength matters. And always will.

Share your foxhole (your place in the world) with someone who can fight like the devil. Embrace them close. Support them, too, for it's your comrades that will keep you alive, keep you going when you want to give up, and if you are lucky enough to have them in your foxhole, you will survive and be a much better person for it.

"The young man knows the rules, but the old man knows the exceptions." — *Oliver Wendell Holmes, Sr.*

★ RULE 25

Obey the rules of the game. Be the best at following them. Break the rules when doing so supports the central purpose of those rules.

There is a principle in life that says we should obey the rules of the game; moral rules, community norms, family customs, and laws and regulations. Rules are most effective at pointing to what we believe is of significant value (like this book). Otherwise, why would we have rules? Rules help create stability and predictability, improve efficiency, and build a safer place to work and play. Rules protect the weak and generate a more level playing field in our lives. Good advice is to be the best at following the rules; know what they are, why they exist, and how those rules function. Find it within yourself to be a cheerleader for rules and learn to improve upon them when reasonable, and you can muster agreement among others. The act of following rules and refining and improving rules gain you respect and admiration among the many in your group.

We also see those people who carefully and expertly follow the rules. These are the folks who are leaders and successful in our community, at church, in school, at the workplace, in the political sphere, and on the field of sports. We find them admirable and look to them as models of virtue. We copy their rule-following behavior. Who does not want to be someone upheld in the highest esteem by others? We see people who follow the rules diligently as examples of decency and admiration. Rule following is also a form of communication. It tells us what is essential and of value; recklessness versus safety, bad manners versus good, immoral behavior versus honesty. Follow the rules and be the best at following them. You will be content in doing so, and you will be an upstanding member of your community.

But there are also times to break the rules. True enough, we are suspicious of those who are drone-like in their subservience to rules. Rigid adherence to rules shows a lack of creativity, flexibility, and intellect. Rules exist within a pecking order of rules, like the rules of playing a single baseball game, to be contrasted with the rules of the entire baseball season. The latter rules that govern the game, what we call meta-rules (or rules about rules), embody the central core of the game's purpose.

Meta rules represent a higher-order principle that overlays all other rules. For example, they say in baseball that you can win all the [individual] games but still lose that season's victory pennant. Know the meta-rules. And yet to know them requires a higher level of awareness. We all can implicitly understand this; even children appreciate it. Kids know that if they win all the games, other children will stop playing with them. The meta-rule is "play the game."

Follow the rules, understand the rules, and be an advocate for the rules. Follow the rules except when doing so undermines the central purpose of those same rules.

"Of what use is a philosopher who doesn't hurt anybody's feelings? – Diogenes

★ **RULE 26**

Your feelings don't matter; pull up your big-boy pants and grow a pair!

You hear this a lot in the U.S. military, "Your feelings don't matter." On my first Infantry unit assignment, the Sergeants had us running around the barracks, carrying our footlockers and screaming as loud as possible, "My feelings don't matter." They taught us something important about soldiering and being an adult; sometimes, your feelings really don't matter.

Of course, I look back on that time with the U.S. Army Infantry's finest with some trepidation. Would I want to go through this primeval-like initiation into the U.S. Army again? Nope! But I'm glad I did. All of us there will admit that Infantry training was realistic and the hardest thing we had ever done. Many in our unit cracked under mental pressure. They were taken away, never to return.

Technically speaking, your feelings do matter … but only a little. Feelings can be a motivator; in that respect, feelings do matter. But Army NCOs that train Soldiers don't care one whit about our feelings, prior girlfriends, our religion, the color of our skin, or where we came from. We were army green to those Sergeants training us, and their job was to show us how to be a Soldier.

It's tough. Learning that your feelings don't matter will come as a shock. At first, the idea is difficult to accept. We've all been taught that our feelings are important. Our moms were wonderful, and we do love our moms; she told us we were the best, and she went out of her way to protect our feelings. Then again, we should also learn that our feelings can work against our success as an adult in school or the workplace

Army and Marine Sergeants have a way with words that hit home for many of us Privates. One day, the young mosquito stripper (Private E-2), standing at the position of attention, asked our Squad Leader about getting a little time to "collect himself." Standing next to us was the meanest-looking, fiercest Sergeant ever. He scared the daylights out of us. Staff Sergeant Charlie "Caboose" Crusher (don't ever call him "Caboose"), one tough SOB, just looked at us and said, "Hey, maggots! Time for you lovely ladies to go on a five-mile run in full combat gear." He loved calling us "ladies" to tell us we were not up to his soldiering standards. There is nothing like mass punishment to get your attention.

"Take that hill." Our first squad-level exercise was about to happen, and we were to be graded on our ability to take a hill away from the "enemy." Our Squad Leader was good for us. He taught us to be tough, detailed-oriented, and single-minded in accomplishing our mission. At Fort Polk, it was Hill 937 (named after the infamous Battle of Hamburger Hill in the Vietnam War). That day did not go well. Our "attack" to take Hill 937 was late starting and not synchronized with an adjacent squad. We miserably failed the exercise but what happened after was something to remember. Staff Sergeant Crusher was in rare form. Just leave it there for your imagination. At the end of the squad training exercise, our arm muscles were stronger from doing thousands of punishment pushups.

Do your feelings matter? Nope, your feelings don't matter, at least not to all the adults in the room.

"We are all born ignorant, but one must work hard to remain stupid." – Benjamin Franklin

★ **RULE 27**

Don't do stupid. And stop acting like a child. When you pull the pin, Mr. Grenade is NOT your friend.

We all know a good idea when we hear it, but stupid ideas linger much longer than they should. Stupid ideas are those that are silly or illogical, or unworkable. Stupid ideas can get you killed. "Don't buy that BB gun; you'll shoot your eye out." Sounds a lot like our mothers giving us some damn good advice. As children, we probably ignored what she had to say. Parents are keen on their kids not doing stupid stuff; they've been there and know. It's a good idea to listen to those with experience; you show respect and trust in them when you listen. Fail to listen means you are prone to fail, on occasion failing spectacularly

Some folks will tell you this rule of what-not-to-do (aka, don't do stupid) is plain old common sense. Let's be clear! It is not common sense. On the battlefield, you can witness some of the dumbest behavior, and it's impressive they are still alive. Occasionally, I met some who were likely to place prominently in the Darwin Awards category. This award is a tongue-in-cheek honor recognizing those who contributed to human evolution. They do this by removing themselves from the gene pool by dying through their own acts. Things you and I would never try; they seem to admire and revere. Here is a bonus, some of them are alive to talk about it. Lucky them!

Here are a few stupid things I witnessed in combat. There are many more, but you get the idea:

1. Going into combat without ammunition or grenades.
2. A rifle fouled with carbon, and you cannot chamber a round.
3. Traveling in a vehicle low on fuel.
4. Removing the bullet-proof armor plate to "lighten up."
5. Hiding your battle buddy's ammo as a joke.
6. Walking in the tall grass along the roadside (explosive landmines are hidden there).
7. Not knowing your location. Or where the enemy is.
8. Thinking you're Superman and drawing enemy fire.
9. Believing a hand grenade's 5-second fuse lasts 5 seconds. When you pull the pin, Mr. Grenade is NOT your friend.
10. Thinking the Horse Cavalry will come riding in with their bugles blowing when you're in trouble.

Anyone interested in beginning their career as a comedian should be confident that there is plenty of material about people doing stupid things. People do stupid stuff, and they are great at making us smile while they fail. It's also great for learning how to be a better person. Admit your action was stupid, learn from it, and don't do it again. Also, laugh a little about it too.

When I was a new kid in Junior High School, the local bully said to meet him behind the gym after school for some "new guy schooling." I was there on time, expecting a fair one-on-one fight. I was slightly annoyed when three boys larger than me jumped in to help the bully. Yes, I got beat up because I thought the bully would come alone to a fight. Don't make assumptions either; that's just as stupid. Assumptions can get you the Darwin Award too.

If you find yourself doing something stupid, just stop. My grandmother (we called her bigmama) always said that one day we might find ourselves doing something stupid. There will be times when you still find yourself in a hole. Just be sure you don't make things worse for yourself; stop digging. Sounds like practical advice? It should!

Don't do stupid. And please stop acting like a child. It's embarrassing.

"Waste no more time arguing about what a good man should be. Be one." – Marcus Aurelius

★ **RULE 28**

Stop wasting your life. Orient your life in every possible way to increase your chances that what you want will occur.

Wasting time is doing anything that does not contribute to your personal goals. Know your goals and where you're going. And if you are willing to make the right sacrifices to get there, you will always be successful.

Psychologists tell us that people typically operate at about half their total capacity. Their studies indicate that most folks waste about four to six hours daily. That's one hell of a lot of time being thrown away, which we could have put to better use. We can all agree that using our lives for more productive activities is a step toward a more fulfilling life.

We waste our time watching television, playing video games, drinking and drugging ourselves into a stupor, and we know what wasted time is about. We know we're doing it. We're fully conscious of it. And, the younger you are, the more negative impact wasted time has on you throughout your life because your youth is the exact time for you to invest in your future.

One meaningful way to stop wasting your life is to learn to write. There is no difference between writing and thinking. Those who can write will succeed in life at several magnitudes greater than everyone else. Start writing, even if it is imperfect, even if it is terrible writing with lousy grammar and bad sentence structure. You need to learn to write because writing forces you to think, which makes you act correctly and successfully. If you practice writing now, in five years, you will be so far ahead of your peers that they will never catch up.

Also, make a schedule and stick to it. Schedules are used to plan the day, not as a straightjacket to tie you down. Most of us don't like following a schedule because we make it too restrictive. That is wrong. A schedule is not a list of responsibilities; it is a manageable layout of those things you want to do that day. Set up your day as if it were the best possible day you could realistically create. The rule is that you should be better off by the end of that day than you were at the beginning. Ultimately, your schedule is a negotiation with yourself to trade work today for a payoff tomorrow.

Reject making things consciously worse for yourself and others. We all do this, and we do it because there are times we are spiteful, resentful, arrogant, or deceitful. Get your act together. It isn't only your life; it's the fate of everyone you've networked with. The things you do or don't do are far more critical than you think.

The alternative is a meaningless life with no responsibility. You can then whine about your suffering and disastrous life; maybe the only thing you gain from it is that people will feel sorry for you. Taking this pathway as a martyr and rejecting responsibility (with its associated difficulties) is the wrong path. To live a harmful life, you harm your family, and if enough people do that, then it's hell on earth. Bear your burden of life properly, live with your head up, and be confident in yourself and others.

Furthermore, no one can live well without a routine. I recommend you get a routine because you cannot be mentally healthy without it. You need to pick a time to get up (preferably early in the morning), go to bed, and stick to it. Otherwise, you will screw up your circadian rhythms that regulate your mood. Any mood other than being positive works against you.

Plan the life you would like to have and do that by having a conversation with yourself. Present to yourself the idea that you want a good life (not an easy task). Doing so may sound irresponsible, but some people don't like themselves very much. Consequently, they beat themselves up for not fulfilling their daily needs and then doing nothing about it. This is such a pathetic way to spend your day. One of the main reasons people don't get what they want is that they don't figure out what they want. The probability of getting what you want when you don't specify your goals is precisely zero. You will fail. Figure out what you want and aim at it (RULE 4: Aim high, find your mission in life).

Take the time to reorient your life in every possible way to increase your chance that what you want will occur. If you are willing to live in the world properly, not waste your time, and know your goal and aim at it, you will be more than you can be.

Stop wasting your life.

"Judge a man by his questions rather than by his answers." –
Voltaire

★ **RULE 29**

Ask the right questions; there are too many dumb questions.

We often hear that there is no such thing as a dumb question. That is not true. Plenty of dumb and embarrassing questions make adults look foolish and uninformed. There are many advantages to asking good questions; don't squander the opportunity. Stupid questions always happen and can be misinterpreted, irritate people, waste time and resources, and tarnish your credibility. When you aren't focused, what you say can become a bad question for all to hear, and you will wonder whether you are intellectually up to the task.

The ability to ask relevant questions is a talent of good listeners. Such questions, asked skillfully, can do two things to enhance communication. They can elicit useful information to fill in knowledge gaps, usually to improve your decision-making. In addition, good questions can help verify existing information, ensuring confidence in what we already know. Good questions encourage intelligent thinking, inspire people to think in new ways, expand their vision range, and enable them to contribute more. It shows that we care, demonstrate respect, and produce courteous behavior.

There are many ways to ask a good question, one that both goes to the heart of the subject being discussed and allows others to judge the person asking the question. Always ask questions that force the other person to stop for a moment and think hard before answering. Such questions will provide you with several advantages.

Here are a few words of advice from military mentors. First, only ask essential questions. Second, don't interrupt once you ask a question. Third, speak your listener's language. Lastly, plan your questions ahead so they are clear, make sense, and show you have command of the subject. Review and analyze your question and ask yourself how it could be asked in a better way. Remember that the most successful among us are those who ask good questions, listen intently to the answers, and incorporate this information learned into your actions.

Practice asking good questions daily and with care. It gets easier over time. Ask the right questions; there are too many dumb questions.

"Great things are not accomplished by those who yield to trends and fads and popular opinion." — *Jack Kerouac*

★ **RULE 30**

Don't be swayed by fashion, fads, or promises of fun.

Driving with my 15-year-old in the car and listening to the radio was great for our father-daughter relationship. We got to talk, relax, and see the Pennsylvania countryside. I'd purposefully selected a radio station that played music appealing to teenagers. Playing on the radio was a song by the Spice Girls, a famous British singing group. My daughter, Audrey, spoke up and said, "Hey, dad, why are you listening to oldies from the 90s?" Audrey was about to introduce me to popular music groups and teenager fashions and fads. Most of what she said was innocent, thank goodness.

The Spice Girls' music is fun to listen to. It's harmless and mindless but appealing because it is rebellious in spirit. That is why it is so enticing to the young. In my teenage years, the Beatles' British singing group was popular, the pet rock was the thing, and tie-dye t-shirts and banana-seat bicycles were groovy. Harmless? Yes. But there were also several sinister fashions, fads, and promises of fun. Dangerous drugs continuously evolve with promises of low-cost fun and enlightenment. Alcohol remains a great escape and destroyer of human lives. And many modern ideologies, like Communism, promise instant solutions to all our problems, and utopia is just around the corner.

Fashionable causes, fads, and promises of fun are tempting. They promise much and require little responsibility to accomplish anything other than voicing your support. Some are supported by ideologies that tell us we are morally superior to those not with our cause; that makes us feel good. You can show your superiority through virtue signaling, a public expression of your opinion to show your moral correctness. This can be accomplished through social media, purchasing pre-approved products, affinity with historical victim groups, shaming non-believers, suppression of free speech, and groupthink. The danger is evident to those who study history. The 20th century provides stark lessons in how fashionable ideas turn out when in the hands of evil people.

Don't be swayed by fashion, fads, or promises of fun.

OUTTAKE: Winning every game is not winning

Growing up, baseball was our game. Every boy in school played it. We all played on a Little League team. We enjoyed pick-up baseball in the streets and even while running through the backyards of our neighborhood. Sometimes we won, and sometimes we lost. My dad's advice was, "It's not whether you win or lose, but how you play the game."

At the time, I didn't understand this piece of wisdom. And this is a very ancient idea. I gave my son the same advice. His question, "What do you mean by that?" The advice was correct, but it was difficult to say why. Maybe it had to do with just following the rules and being kind to the other players. Wrong.

A game is not just a game. A game is part of a series of games (even when playing with friends). Winning a baseball game was not really what we wanted (although we certainly thought so). Our aim was to win the baseball season championship, and that was the result of a series of games.

Winning the championship and winning a game are not the same thing. And the strategy for winning a championship and a single game is not the same. If you only play a single game, it might be better for your best player to make all the critical plays. For the championship, it is more important that the team acts as a team. These are different strategies because the striving for the championship occurs across time and with different competitors.

As good parents, we should not try to teach our kids to win a single game. We should be teaching them how to win the championship. So, a championship is much closer to real life.

Real life, however, might be a whole series of championships. Teach your children to be a proper competitors in an entire series of games. You do that by helping them develop their character. A mature character is the best strategy to help your kids win the championship (or a series of championships in life) over the largest span of time.

Teach your children not to win exactly but to play well with others. Yes, try to win. But they should also strive to develop the talents of those around them and not make it about winning all things all the time. This makes your kids fun to play with. If your son or daughter is fun to play with, then other kids are there to play with them, and adults want to teach them.

During their lifetime, your kids will be given more opportunities to play baseball (or whatever sport or life's endeavor); this is how they will win in life. They keep getting invited to play more games. They get more opportunities. This is why teaching your kids that winning a baseball game is not everything. Knowing this is a strategy for doing well in life. Do not sacrifice your ability to win in life; winning a single game is not the point.

This is why selfish professional ball players are not appreciated. Yes, they are winners. But their character is suspect. They are "winners" in the most narrow sense. That is because we are looking for those that can win across a set of games. Fans watching these games have a much more negative response if a self-centered player loses and then complains about the loss. Why? Because that player's character is suspect.

The greatest athletes are those who can lose gracefully. They are not only exceptionally skilled at what they do, but they are trying to expand their skills at all times (increasing their chances of winning in the future). This kind of behavior is what people like to watch. We don't like watching the perfect athlete, but the athlete who is getting better and helping teammates get better.

If a player loses a game and then whines about it, that player has sacrificed the more important principle of constantly improving their skills. Instead, the player should analyze where the game was lost and not blame it on the team or the referees. If they complain, those players are not pushing themselves to be better.

Help the other players on your team. Don't grandstand. If you have the opportunity to beat your opponent by crushing them, it is wise not to do so and not humiliate them. What you should want is for the best in others. And that is what you want from those who surround you. They will hold you to a higher standard if you have those kinds of folks around you.

If for some reason, any reason, you do not uphold the highest performance or the best character, these people will immediately react to correct you. They will tell you that you are demeaning yourself. You are less than you could be, and you won't like that. There is honest judgment in that, and it's harsh. Be with people who genuinely want the best for you and are willing to improve you.

Play nobly. Pay attention to your teammates. Winning every game is not winning.

"Families, friends and communities often find a source of courage rising up from within. Indeed, sadly, it seems that it is tragedy that often draws out the most and the best from the human spirit."   *– Queen Elizabeth II*

★ **RULE 31**

Always attend Funerals. Do the right thing even when you don't want to.

My brother Philip and I stood there, looking at the casket of our great-grandfather. This was the first funeral we ever attended. Neither of us wanted to be there. My father made it clear, "You're going to the funeral." I couldn't talk, my brother cried, and we were both in shock from looking at the faces of our relatives and strangers. Years later, people would remember the two little boys and note that we were the only two children present. We learned a life lesson; do the right thing.

Even when you don't want to do the right thing, or it is unpopular, or everyone laughs at you, or you stand alone, no one will support you. Doing the right thing is a sign of emotional maturity. Attending a funeral may not mean much to you, but it sure means a lot to someone else. Is it inconvenient? Yes. Is attending a funeral awkward and uncomfortable? Yes. There is nothing heroic or brave in attending a funeral, but it is something we must do. Being present among the deceased person's relatives and friends at the funeral shows respect and honors the person who has passed.

I attend many memorial services and funerals in the military, literally hundreds of them. That was the sad part of the job, but I went, not because of an obligation or career requirement but because it was right. Many parents, spouses, and various relatives and friends of the deceased expressed appreciation for the time taken to be there.

Inevitably, there are tragedies in life. They are unavoidable; the death of a loved one, terminal cancer, serious injury, etc. As free human beings, we have two primary choices in the face of tragedy. One is the nihilist approach, which would have us believe there is nothing to do but accept a world destined for heartbreak. The other is to be the most dependable person for others, to help settle the tragedy. Humans have been dealing with death forever. We are descendants of those who could manage it. Attend the funeral, and be the one others can depend on; this is the way to make a bad situation less dreadful. Courage and nobility in the face of tragedy are what is necessary. In this way, we honor those who have passed away and stand firm with their loved ones.

Many years ago, my Engineer unit deployed at the beginning of the Iraq War; it was a time of great personal difficulty. It was also the first time I had good friends killed in combat. One morning four of our best friends were there, and we talked and laughed; a few hours later, they were dead in a helicopter shoot-down. Eleven Soldiers died in that encounter; four were long-time friends. Those present at funerals and memorials do so to honor those who have died, regardless of the cause of death or inconvenience of attendance.

Always go to the funeral. Always do the right thing.

"Pursue your dreams but have a backup plan." – Kane

★ RULE 32

Always have a backup plan; the enemy has theirs.

Combat-proven leaders know that the original plan never survives contact with the enemy, so it best be ready with an alternative to accomplishing the mission. This means you should be prepared with a backup plan. Have a Plan B, and possibly also a Plan C. This truism is not new; too many learned the hard way and had another plan, just in case. Failure will happen; it is best to be ready. Unsurprisingly, people frequently fail to have a backup. Whether due to intellectual laziness, a lack of brains, or insufficient time and resources to plan, it matters little except that we can learn from this kind of self-inflicted failure. Having no backup plan signifies the person is not ready for greater responsibilities. Opportunities will pass them by, and they will not even know it.

One method of learning how to be effective is to discuss what some other successful person planned to do if their plans had gone awry. If there is a detailed and workable solution, you are speaking with someone who will be successful at the end of the day. If there is no backup or one that is only sketchy in details, expect this person not to last. Even the Boy Scout motto directly applies this idea: "be prepared." As part of their training, the individual scout is taught to be in a constant state of readiness. And they are good at making a backup plan.

The fact that Boy Scout founder Robert Baden-Powell ensured that boys were taught leadership essentials is impressive. Leaders in our modern and complex society should be at least as diligent as those Scouts. They should have prepared themselves and organized into a state of readiness. Without a reasonable and workable backup plan, figure that when the unexpected happens, panic will set in. That kind of unavoidable failure is unfortunate.

Have a backup plan. Your enemy already has theirs. Don't get caught flat-footed when you could have easily avoided unexpected surprises.

"I have a dream that my four little children will one day live in a nation where they will not be judged by the color of their skin but by the content of their character." – Reverend Martin Luther King, Jr.

★ RULE 33

You will be harshly judged by others who know nothing. Get over it. And do not judge yourself compared to someone else; it will disappoint and frustrate you and make you anxious, resentful, and unhappy. Compare yourself today to who you were yesterday.

From the time we are infants, we know that others judge us. Babies can smile, look their mother in her eyes, and coo; even they can judge, albeit primitively. Being judged is a fact of life that permeates our social fabric till the day we die. The harsh reality is that others will harshly judge us, and they will know nothing of importance about us. Humans are judgmental creatures. This process is an outgrowth of the evolutionary process of survival. To judge what is dangerous or safe, poisonous or eatable, bad or good is the ability to live another day. It is an incredibly useful process that has been socially honed to an unbelievable level of value.

To be judged is to see ourselves in the eyes of others, and what we see may surprise us, make us smile, proud, cheerful or anxious, resentful, or unhappy. We react to their judgment and look to ourselves as something worthy or not; that reaction is at the most base emotional level. We all react similarly. Having tough skin can help, but we will still have that instinctive reaction. Move away from here. If you want to be more independent and satisfied with your life, judge yourself today compared to who you were yesterday, not to someone else.

We are at our best when we strive to improve ourselves. In that way, we are not dependent upon others, we are not pulling at the shoestrings of our community, and we have rejected the siren call for pessimism. This is why we need a noble aim in our life, and only then can we judge ourselves properly as we compare who we were yesterday to who we are today. That is the measure of progress and the path to victory over all adverse circumstances.

For these reasons, we should take great care in the judgment of others. Understand why we do so, know that it has great utility, and know that we are human and frequently wrong. Improper judgment is the curse of our existence; we often judge without proper contemplation, logic, careful observation, analysis, or fairness. Judge others, not by their physical traits or the deeds of their ancestors; judge them by their ideas with facts and evidence, not emotion. Judge them by the content of their character.

You will be harshly judged by others who know nothing. Get over it.

"It doesn't take a hero to order men into battle. It takes a hero to be one of those men who goes into battle." – Norman Schwarzkopf

★ RULE 34

Tell stories of heroes and their deeds.

You advance the human spirit when telling a story. Stories have been told since humans walked on the wild plains of Africa long ago. And they continue being told because stories help us formulate and seek out who we are and where we are going. Stories of heroes, like many who rise to the top of their culture and become famous, resonate every time they are told. Something about the stories of heroes and their deeds holds our attention and makes us sit up and notice. We are drawn to heroes because we see ourselves reflected in them. We understand others and ourselves better through these stories and can speak about those wants and desires that help our family and community.

The best stories are universal; they resonate across cultures and across time. They educate us on morality, shape our perspectives, understanding of others, and teach us to act wisely and comprehend our world properly. Without these stories, we are not truly human. It should be no surprise that the bestselling book of all time is the Bible. Why is it a bestseller? The Bible is a series of humanity's most remarkable stories told end to end. These stories came about in the days before the written word and bubbled up as the most useful and explanatory of our existence. Meta-stories, as these much-loved stories are often called, are those stories that compete with others and survive the long road of history.

Lessons are taught through stories, the same way ancient civilizations pass along lessons of the past. Those lessons do not change, even if the story changes. One of the more common hero stories is of St. George and the Dragon. The story is vital for those of us who try to improve upon our own character because it gives insight into those attributes that define greatness: courage, selflessness, steadfastness, and trust, to name a few. St. George is the first story or a variation of that story that many of us remember since we were small children.

According to legends, St. George rescued a princess about to become dinner for a Dragon. By a stroke of luck, St. George was passing through and saved her by beheading the Dragon. A tale of a noble Christian soldier in shining armor coming to the rescue of a princess fits effortlessly with the notions of chivalry and courtly love, which became the driving ethos behind Western ideas of civility and social order.

Not all war heroes are soldiers. By 1943, Italy was out of the war after suffering a series of humiliating by the Allied powers. Italians disposed of the "Duce" Dictator Mussolini and freed all captured Allied POWs. Of course, Hitler was furious at the Italian people's betrayal and retaliated by invading Italy, occupying much of its territory. The POWs were at risk of being recaptured and possibly executed. Catholic Monsignor Hugh O'Flaherty, an Irishman headquartered at the Vatican in Rome, decided to help. Estimates vary, but most believe O'Flaherty and his group hid over 6,500 former POWs and Jews. The Germans quickly discovered that Monsignor O'Flaherty was at the center of it all and banned him from traveling outside the Vatican, under threat of execution. Nevertheless, he did so, dressed in various disguises and earning him the nickname "The Scarlet Pimpernel of the Vatican."

The hero's journey is a standard template of stories that involve a hero who goes on an adventure, is victorious in a decisive crisis and comes home changed or transformed. Everyone loves a story of survival and victory. But why we have heroes is much more. We have heroes because we need them. Heroes reveal our missing qualities and show us the way to emancipation from the straightjacket of culture. Heroes are there to give us hope; perhaps we can be more like them when the going gets tough and others melt away. Heroes validate our moral view of life and remind us of the fragility of life.

Furthermore, heroes are dramatic; they are entertaining in their stories and provide us with a feeling of comfort. Heroes deliver justice with jurisprudence and with fairness. And heroes nurture our deep thoughts of doing good acts for our fellow human beings. Without heroes, we would be lost in a world of evolving standards of morality and arbitrary laws.

It is no accident in history that stories of heroes must be told. They anchor us to our culture and other people just like us. Learn those stories and learn to tell them well. By telling stories of heroes we love so much, we are speaking about the struggles to overcome life's obstacles (the Dragons). In doing so, we loudly demonstrate those very noble ideas we desperately need for self-worth.

Tell stories of heroes and their deeds.

"Hell is paved with good intentions."   —
Bernard of Clairvaux

★ **RULE 35**

Good intentions alone are only the beginning; they must be accompanied by proper action. Intent and results matter. Likewise, if you succeed and do not have good intentions, your efforts are corrupt and will fail.

Life is about living morally and graciously, playing the game and winning by the rules, being a man or woman for others, unselfishly following the unpopular and sometimes difficult path, and knowing when to step up and be counted. These are the actions we see so often displayed as physical and moral courage in the face of danger. People see us and judge us on the outcome of our actions as well as our intent – good or bad. Good intentions mean there is a moral basis for them, but they must also be accompanied by proper action.

And, if you make it and do not have good intentions, your efforts will be corrupt and eventually fail. Already, we humans are prone to corruption. Corruption of our character is easy; we get to lie, cheat, steal, betray, be resentful, and do nothing difficult. We look for justifications for not having good intent because that is much less effort. We would prefer being willfully blind to the dangers ahead. If something difficult comes along, and you have allowed your character to become corrupted, your actions will not be for the benefit of others. It cannot. From corruption, no good act can come.

That is why good character matters. And it is immoral to use the excuse of good intent for not taking the correct action. It also does not mean that good intent naturally leads to good acts. Know the difference between right and wrong, learn to identify evil when you see it, and be prepared for obstacles in your way. Action, the right, moral, ethical action, is required of you.

Rarely will we possess all the resources, permissions, knowledge, and skills to get things done the right way. That is why developing our character, proper relationships and networks, creating trust and confidence in others, and influencing people to achieve more incredible things is such a noble goal. Good people get things done. They do so ethically, legally, and by taking care of people. They aspire to loyalty through tough times and good. They have what is called "gravitas!" The road to hell may be paved with good intentions, but the potholes will not be repaired without the right actions

Life is competition. Life is survival. But it is also much more! Good intentions alone are only the beginning; they must be accompanied by proper action. And avoid corrupting your character, for what you do will not be sufficient and is destined to fail.

"Power is no blessing in itself, except when it is used to protect the innocent." – Jonathan Swift

★ **RULE 36**

Protect the weak and innocent; never pick on the less fortunate; it's immoral. Don't antagonize the strong without cause; it's stupid.

We all like to do what we can to help those in need, those who are down and out, and those who are destitute. Being good is giving back to your community and assisting those who require help to survive. When things go wrong, we look to someone who will step up to slay the Dragon, rescue the maiden, and live happily ever after. This story is symbolic of human existence and tells us our place in life is not easy but that we must fight for it. To do so, you must be ready to protect the weak and innocent.

Like any athlete on the playing field, religious leader, police officer, or employee at a difficult job, having the right moral character and physical strength makes all the difference between failure and success. That is why you must have the skills and experience, the right tools and knowledge, motivation, and courage. If you lack these, you are doomed to failure.

The world is littered with the bodies of tormentors, bullies, and evil tyrants who target those who are less fortunate than us. To be successful, I believe, means you must do two things. First, you must not be weak, unimaginative, lazy, or spiritless. Second, you must protect those who are weak and innocent. How to do that is the challenge. It would be best to adopt a high degree of discipline, boldness in your actions, and elegance in carrying them out. It means telling the truth and not being fooled by pseudo-truths or taken in by propaganda. This way, we can see evil for what it is, making us powerful, physically strong, mentally resilient, spiritual, and devoted to our family, community, and country.

You will be admired if you can do this. Your life will not be easy, far from it. You will be continuously challenged. But only through overcoming the greatest of challenges can you be successful.

In addition, do not antagonize the strong without cause, or anyone for that matter. That kind of behavior is not just stupid but morally corrupt. Be an outstanding citizen for others. The Jesuits have it right. "Men for others" is their philosophy, and they deserve our support. Students in schools run by Jesuits are instructed hundreds of times to become community leaders. This idea is defined in Jesuit priest Pedro Arrupe's ideal of "men for others." Now in their co-ed schools, it has changed to "men and women for others." Still, it's honest and direct.

Seek the path to that which is moral and good. To do this is the way to a life of fulfillment and virtue. There is no higher calling than to protect the weak and the innocent. There will be hell for those who refuse to help them.

Protect the weak and innocent; never pick on the less fortunate; it's immoral.

"Look at a day when you are supremely satisfied at the end. It's not a day when you lounge around doing nothing; it's when you've had everything to do, and you've done it." – Margaret Thatcher

★ RULE 37

Never complain, be part of the solution; nobody likes a whiner.

As a company-grade Army officer, I had the privilege of having several hard-hitting old Platoon Sergeants working for me. We were more than fortunate to have them on our team, and all the young Soldiers learned a great deal from their experiences. One day, Sergeant First Class Roger Andrews found me complaining about the Mess Hall food – like all Soldiers typically do – and made it clear that good men never complain. He said, "Good men are always part of the solution."

Later that week, I was assigned to be the Food Service Officer. That meant extra duty, responsible for overseeing all dining facility operations. There was much to learn from that point on; details of food storage, preparation, serving, disposal, and sanitation were at the top of the list. That duty position ensures every Soldier is served a nutritious meal and that it is served anywhere, anytime, and any place in the world and in an organization with a mission to go into combat on short notice.

You should never complain because we all have the responsibility to do something to correct problems, even when not our direct responsibility. Platoon Sergeant Andrews said that only children have a right to complain – some call it whining – because they have no power and control over their situation; grown-ups who whine have never grown up. Good point.

Complaining is an immature reaction to events. It is irrelevant that a problem is not within your control. When you complain, you have regressed to childishness. Anyone who complains is simply not doing their best. Everyone who witnesses someone complaining knows it too. That is why we have a duty to choose our words carefully so that we don't appear to be complaining and being viewed as a juvenile.

For example, we have all witnessed politicians who complain about a variety of things. Their actions, however, speak loudly. Rarely do politicians do something meaningful that resolves a problem or issue, but they are big complainers. On the other hand, military leaders of the past were experts at fixing things and not complaining. It is also no surprise that when the American public rated their confidence in each institution, the military exceeded politicians in all measures of trust and confidence.

Platoon Sergeant Andrews was superb – a true man's man and leader – and it was sad to see him retire after nearly 30 years of military service to the nation. What he knew and his ability to mentor others were superb. All of us were better off for knowing him; we learned and took his ideas to our hearts that if you want to succeed, don't whine. Do something that will fix the problem. Lesson learned!

Never complain, be part of the solution. Nobody likes a whiner.

"I am not afraid of an army of lions led by a sheep; I am afraid of an army of sheep led by a lion." — *Alexander the Great*

★ **RULE 38**

Be like a Lion; that way, you walk with the awareness that nobody will mess with you. Stand up straight. Look directly ahead, and you will be feared. Learn to defend yourself in a fistfight and against others with weapons.

Be like a Lion; dangerous, courageous, willing to fight, a hunter, and perhaps someday, a leader of the pack. Put away your smartphone. Stop hunching over and looking at your text messages. Give up your video games. Stand up straight with your shoulders back. Sit up properly. Good posture will help put you on the upward curve, and others will notice that you might be more than they think. Hunching over invites more bullying; people will see you as uninteresting and plain, you are less likely to go on an adventure, no one will want you on their team, and others will think of you as powerless, weak, and unimportant. Don't be a frozen rabbit when the world comes knocking at your door (opportunity knocks). Remember that you are the one in control. Be ready to answer it with your eyes open, and maybe you can take advantage of whatever is brought to you.

Being like a Lion is being competent. Be prepared to say to the world, "Bring it on. I can handle it." Yes, legitimately, there are good reasons not to. Fine, but your objective should be to handle it, no matter what it is and do so voluntarily and courageously. And if you can do this, you can now transcend life's tragedies. We know this because people admire and respect those who are competent. We promote them and raise them up as ideals of excellence within our community. Nothing is more powerful than competence; everything we do and every sphere of living is fundamentally based on competence.

A reasonable goal, a place where we can see this in action, is to be the most reliable person at a funeral. Everyone at a funeral is emotionally broken and you adding to that misery is not good. You will be grieving, certainly, but this is a time to step up with some character. It's bad enough that someone has died; that's tragic, but making it worse is no answer. Be that person people can come to. Be strong. Folks need strength most in the midst of tragedy. Be that person. It takes courage.

Push yourself to rid yourself of those traits that make you weaker. This will help nurture personal growth and is what makes you useful. If you do that, you get the joy of participating more with others and the confidence that you are building yourself stronger simultaneously. Accept responsibility. Life is difficult. And staring at danger is likewise hard. But that is how we can be a better person, just a little each day, and in a week, a month, or a year, we will be far better, less worthless, less afraid, and less vulnerable.

Aim at being a Lion; that way you walk with the awareness that nobody will mess with you.

"In the long history of humankind (and animal kind, too), those who learned to collaborate and improvise most effectively have prevailed." — *Charles Darwin*

★ **RULE 39**

Keep your eye on the ball; be vigilant. See the enemy first; that's how you become their final solution.

Pay close attention to what is happening around you and, as well, note what is not happening that should be occurring. Know your surroundings, what is ordinarily present, who frequents where you are, how people typically act, and the importance of your presence. Be aware and always vigilant; one day, you will be called upon to step into the breach and save lives, property, or things of great value. To be vigilant, you must possess the indispensable traits of persistence, presence, and patience.

We all struggle to remain focused over the long term. That is why we connect ourselves to teams of people we can trust and those who have confidence in us; there should always be those on your team who are on alert. Our greatest downfall is complacency as we look away. It's natural to do so; beware. One early morning, our convoy from the Baghdad Airport to the Green Zone was traveling over Route Irish, often called "the most dangerous stretch of highway on Earth." Our rear security vehicle guard (in an armored Humvee) allowed a civilian vehicle to pass us in violation of standard procedures. As the civilian vehicle passed, the suicide bomber exploded next to one of our transports, killing several Soldiers. It was later determined that the rear guard had fallen asleep in the gunner's seat. He had done this job daily for nearly a year and had never before experienced an attack. Complacency, in this case, resulted in the deaths of four Soldiers and many wounded. "Complacency kills," we had been warned.

It is challenging to remain vigilant. Many leaders have achieved accolades for coming to rescue a civilian company from bankruptcy. Nevertheless, the worker who stays with the organization is the real champion because it is that person who ensures things work every day. It is human nature to let one's guard down, to lay back and relax. The difficulty of maintaining a high state of readiness is well known; it is resource intensive. There have been famous battles won when the weak prevailed over a superior force because someone failed to maintain their vigilance.

To Americans, we recall our history when General George Washington led a small band of Minutemen across the Delaware River to attack Trenton, New Jersey, on Christmas night, December 25, 1776. After the nighttime crossing, Washington's forces attacked the Hessian troops (paid auxiliary troops working for the British), surprising them and quickly overwhelming their inadequate defenses. The surprise maneuver and the small victory gave the American colonies a much-needed boost in morale.

Avoiding complacency is a popular pastime in leadership symposiums, and numerous self-help articles and books are written on the subject. A few tips for avoiding complacency are: get a good night's sleep, never assume anything, don't underestimate others, stay focused, and surround yourself with energetic people. Complacency can get you killed (or injured), destroy your career, and screw up your life. Everyone is vulnerable. Don't get comfortable … stay paranoid!

Keep your eye on the ball; be vigilant.

"Bookstores have entire 'self help' sections and not a single 'help others' book." – Simon Sinek

★ RULE 40

Always eat last; that's how you care for others. Show them you care. Never give a reason for others to lose their confidence in you.

One of the least appreciated life lessons is that good leaders eat last. This means that good people forgo their interests to support others on their team. To say "leaders eat last" is symbolic of the notion that the best among us accept responsibility to help people perform their very best.

In the military, I always ate last (literally). Once as an Army Company Commander on a field training exercise at Fort Hood, Texas, there was no food for the last few Soldiers to eat. By eating last, I discovered the cooks had not prepared a sufficient quantity of the meal, and with that knowledge (of hunger), I was motivated to fix the problem … if you don't know a problem exists, you cannot fix it. Eat last to verify your troops have what they need to fight. Put your Soldiers ahead of your personal concerns.

Eating last is also an outward display of how we interact with others. A lot is written about ways to improve ourselves; while this is good, it rarely involves helping others. Author Simon Sinek asks how some organizations consistently do better than others. In one of the most popular TED presentations, he talks about the issue of "Why does your organization exist?" He says they must answer the question "why" to be the best and then put good leaders in charge to make it happen. The most exemplary leaders among us excel at inspiring people. They can rally people for a cause because it is the right thing to do. Therefore, people are inspired not by *what* we do; instead, they are inspired by *why* we do it.

In the military, we know that the Army exists to confront and destroy our nation's enemies. But why do we do it? The better motivating factor for the Soldier is not that we are told to destroy the enemy but why the enemy is a threat to us and thus must be destroyed. This may seem a rather obvious point, but it is most commonly ignored in literature and academics. However, it is not ignored by good leaders who understand what motivates others to action.

The most influential people I know eat last. They know that their team will achieve its mission only by creating an environment for people to excel. That environment is created through communicating what will improve people on our team. Unsurprisingly, some of the most outstanding leaders in history have concisely and consistently communicated this idea.

Always eat last; that's how you care for others.

OUTTAKE: Hey, watch this!

If you're a guy, you've heard this before. One of your good buddies is about to do something "exciting" and probably very stupid. The first time I remember it being said was the day my childhood friend, Wilson, said, "Hey, watch this!" as he jumped about 20 feet off an old trestle railroad bridge. We were about eight years old.

What an adventure! Jumping off a bridge took courage, and we knew it. When Wilson hit the water, he screamed. I panicked. I thought he had died on impact, so I ran to town as fast as possible to gather a rescue party. Young men where I lived all had cars, and they quickly drove me to the old bridge. I looked over the edge to see Wilson below, but he was not there. I thought the Sheriff would throw me in jail; he was one mean SOB.

Earlier that day, I dropped a firecracker into a beer bottle, prepared to throw it as hard as possible. I yelled to Wilson, "Hey, watch this!" We say, "boys will be boys," regardless of age. Boys tend to do stupid things more often than girls or older men. Perhaps that is why the Darwin Award (given to folks who remove themselves from the gene pool) is given more often to young men. There is some entertainment value in hearing stories about such people. Fortunately, the bottle exploded far enough from my face that I didn't get glass in my eyes.

My friend Wilson landed in the river below and promptly broke his right arm. He barely escaped drowning; since he was right-handed, he had to learn to write with his left. To this day, his penmanship is horrible. But we still laugh about the whole affair, which is why we are guys. Our wives had another viewpoint, less funny.

Living, we thought, was about overcoming fear. We knew about the dangers of what we did, and we moved forward anyway. We weren't naïve. We were more alive, fully self-conscious, than ever. We understood our limitations and how we might get hurt. We might have been afraid, but we decided to jump off that bridge anyway.

Wilson and I were always afraid of that trestle bridge. We discovered that fear helped keep us smart about the dangers of jumping off. If we weren't scared, then we might see it as being less dangerous; and that was not true. But by facing our fears, we became braver each time we went there and looked over the edge into the abyss of the river.

We faced our fears. I figured I could have found less dangerous entertainment, but doing something really stupid at that bridge gave us a thrill and a bit of reassurance too. We had courage in ourselves, and that helped us walk with confidence at home and in school. Fortunately, I'm still alive, surviving my childhood only by blind luck. I've got the scars to prove it, and so does Wilson.

"The key is not to prioritize what's on your schedule but to schedule your priorities." — Stephen Covey

★ **RULE 41**

Get scheduled, establish a routine. Achieve your life's goals that you voluntarily create by building a set of smaller sub-tasks to get you there.

A schedule is unbelievably helpful in achieving your life's goals; those goals you create voluntarily. To help reach your goals properly, establish tasks supporting those goals. Every goal could have five or 25 tasks tied to them, so put them into your schedule. Consciously create a workable schedule for you; only you can do it. Make your schedule realistic and attainable. Avoid piling up too many or impossible-to-achieve tasks. And do not create a prison for yourself with the schedule. The objective is to lay out a doable, responsible set of tasks that, if achieved, will lead to your life's goals. This is the way of a winner.

Set up a schedule that would be the best possible day for yourself. It includes a bit of responsibility and reward. The schedule is created so that it allows you to review the day and determine how well you achieved those tasks under each goal. It does not mean that to be better at the end of the day, you have accomplished them all, or even half of them, but that you have completed as many tasks as possible. Today, you may have only accomplished half. Tomorrow, work to achieve more. Do better each day, and do not collapse if you fail one day. The long haul matters and you can succeed by getting better incrementally. Regardless of how small, each step is a move in the right direction. Sometimes, even a wrong step is good if you recognize it and take corrective action. Learn from those mistakes and make them part of your routine to overcome. Don't waste time; follow your schedule.

Using a schedule can be challenging. But it gets easier once you have the motivation to use it daily. This is accomplished through daily routines. Brush your teeth, take a shower, shave, put on clean clothes, and get your mind ready for the day. These are not on a schedule (they could be) but are part of making each day count in a positive way. Make these good habits part of your day. Routines are one of the ways successful people do well. Routines help make us healthier and more efficient, control the day, motivate (less procrastination), and establish consistent expectations of what happens when those routines are followed.

Remember that: 1) You should be better off at the end of the day than yourself at the beginning of that day. 2) Your schedule and routines do not make a slave of you. 3) There is room for flexibility and room to fail. 4) Work, school, family, reading, exercise, and thinking should be balanced with your abilities and needs. 5) The schedule is in writing and posted. This way, you will be motivated and on the road to a productive and good life.

You will find here a typical written schedule (with some recommendations). Remember what you are aiming at – your noble goal. These scheduled tasks should specifically support that life's goal. Work hard at keeping your schedule. This is what is called discipline, and it is not easy. However, the more effort you put into designing a reasonable schedule and following it, the easier it will become.

- Wake up (6 am or before) the same every day
- Exercise (30 minutes)
- Write on a topic of your choosing (15 min.)
- Review the upcoming day's schedule & prepare

- Work or School or other Major Activity
- Lunch (relax if possible, always eat right, do not rush)
- Work or School or other Major Activity
- Reading (15 min.)
- Stretch muscles and Walk (20 min.)
- Write expectations for the following day
- Block time for Family and Friends
- Go to bed early to ensure adequate sleep

A written schedule is more than daily tasks; weekly, monthly, annual, and unscheduled events are also a part of your written schedule. These include items like vehicle maintenance, paying bills, doing the laundry, and grocery shopping. Make sure you include the start time for each task and the approximate time you estimate it takes to complete it.

Routines are smaller tasks you can do that need not be scheduled but must be done correctly and consistently. Things like taking a shower or bath, dressing in clean clothing, house cleaning, and brushing your teeth. You can put these on a "to-do list. Good leaders always use to-do lists, which might also include housework. Some everyday items are not listed here, like watching television, playing video games and going out drinking with your buddies. These should be done with extreme caution, and the less, the better.

Get scheduled, establish a routine.

"One sees great things from the valley; only small things from the peak." – Gilbert K. Chesterton

★ RULE 42

Remember the small things (about others). To us, the small things are unimportant and not worthy of our attention, but to someone else, it could be the most joyful event or issue in their lives. Remember to acknowledge them.

Garbage collector Bob had been in the business all his life. He was older than dirt, pleasant in person, but rugged from working all his life outdoors. Bob was all about running his garbage business and providing for his family. He was to help us re-learn old lessons from our childhood; remember to respect others. The modern name for his job is sanitation worker, but to Bob, what he did was pick up garbage.

Bob would take anything in his garbage truck (some illegal trash might have been picked up). Those days are gone, and so is Bob. But he got things done. Bob kept his distance like he was not as good as the rest of us. He acted like we (his customers) were somehow better than him. Okay, his call. His son, that worked with him, let slip one day that it was Bob's birthday. We gave him one of those new insulated steel mugs that keep your coffee hot, wrapped it in a brown paper bag, and got it ready to give to him later that day when he would be coming by the office on Ft.

Campbell. It was no big deal, a small gift to say thanks. Bob had tears in his eyes. No one, other than his family, had ever recognized his birthday. We talked for a few minutes, and he left. Bob passed away a few weeks later from undiagnosed cancer. Several of us attended his funeral (as we should all do) and met his large, energetic family. They had organized a big party in Bob's memory. Nothing was spared for Bob's shindig, and we were honored guests. Why? Because we did something small (but significant) for Bob. We showed him respect. You just never know.

Remember the small things that are not small to others. Some events in their lives may have no apparent connection to their work or community involvement. We like to minimize these for that reason; our private lives stay private and out of the workplace. We ask ourselves, why would a birthday or a proposal for marriage or graduation from a school affect our performance at work? The standard answer is that these should have no effect, and that would be wrong. The importance of it is not diminished in their lives. Celebrate those events, and show those on your team that you are sufficiently caring so that you can sincerely acknowledge them.

There is a grand lesson here. People are social creatures. They thrive when around others. They seek to be in the company of those they know sincerely value them. What we do and what we say to others matters a great deal. That is why we must carefully decide how we interact. The point is to show others we care and are willing to hold them up publically and say they are essential and not just a cog in the wheel of some giant organization. Remembering the small things generates trust. And trust is the glue that holds relationships together. Loyalty, trustworthiness, courage, and honesty begins here. Support it. Nurture it. Caring about others is at the core of being human.

Always remember to acknowledge the "small" things.

"I start with the premise that the function of leadership is to produce more leaders, not more followers." – Ralph Nader

★ **RULE 43**

Look for successes in others. Don't begrudge their success. Help them achieve success.

You need to know where you are, and it is good to know where others are, too, so that you can praise them for good cause. Like the famous chicken who is going to cross the road. Why does the chicken cross the road? It does so because it assumes there's something better on the other side. You and others are going somewhere slightly better, so that's a good thing. Congratulate the successes of others who have crossed the road to something better.

I became good friends with a man who lived next door while attending college. "Tin-Can" Tommie was his name, and he was one tough dude. He was also attending college. But I remember him for his outlook on life. It went something like this, "Live life knowing that tomorrow you may die." Tin-Can (probably his nickname) was originally a tree logger from southwest Washington state. He drank massive amounts of alcohol, smoked and chewed tobacco, and was a dangerous neighbor. One day, when I wasn't home, he broke into my house (we lived next door in a duplex) because he came home late on one of his regular drinking binges and mistook our house door for his. Never lie to a man like this, so I told him he was wrong and to pay up for the door. He always said to tell him the truth; this is what you always do with dangerous people. I also told him that if I'd been home, I would have shot him when he broke down the door; he smiled. Folks like him can instantly tell when you are lying. And he was always straight with me. He graduated with an Associates Degree in workforce development (whatever that was). My family attended his graduation, and we spoke with several of his professors, thanking them for helping Tin-Can (he appreciated us taking time out of our busy schedule to be there). I'm glad my family lived next door to this dangerous man; he taught us to tell the blunt truth, the whole truth, however difficult it might be, and know that helping others does matter.

When others win, we win too; if we are part of their circle, their world is better, and we are all ahead. However, to begrudge someone an accomplishment is not helpful at all. If you cannot help them across the road, you become an obstacle and a lesser person. Provide that helping hand, even if your help is imperfect, awkward, or weak. Be there for others.

The world is a much better place when we become part of the successes of others, however minuscule. It is built into our biological being; it's about the old ways of protecting the group and survival of the fittest; today, we call it teamwork. We can do this in many ways, like giving moral support and being physically present for them, mentoring/teaching/coaching, or handholding. If we fail to support others, then what happens is we can become frustrated, disappointed, and angry, all those intermingled. Not a good thing. Finding and encouraging success in others becomes a moral obligation required of those who themselves want better from their own lives.

Put your best interests forward, and do not fail to put the best interests of others forward, too, in the broadest sense. Support those interests that are not narrow or self-centered and reject those that only serve the purpose of instant gratification. Doing this is a start in the development of your character and that of others. If you are resentful of others and are in the habit of blaming others for what is wrong in your life, that means you are immature and should grow up. You will not act positively toward what others have rightly accomplished if you are resentful. Do not do this. You want to encourage success, not vilify it. Reject those emotions of unfair treatment, jealousy, abuse, and betrayal. Work to set that right, even in small ways. But, also, stay on top of things and accept the case that you have a moral obligation to others. That is the truth for all humans.

To recognize the success of others, to help them achieve success is a necessary part of your character development and makes you stronger and morally richer over time. And that is an ethical good, a noble goal to reach for, that is worthwhile for you.

Tin-can would agree. And, yes, I would have shot him.

Look for successes in others, and encourage and help them achieve success. Don't begrudge their success.

"You stand up for your teammates. Your loyalty is to them. You protect them through good and bad because they'd do the same for you." – Yogi Berra

★ **RULE 44**

Protect other people's backs. Be loyal. Never betray. And always Check your 6.

The idea of loyalty is as ancient as a human association, although it is often revealed in its opposite (disloyalty, betrayal, ingratitude). The world's greatest thinkers have studied the notion of human commitments, whether to God or each other, and they regard loyalty as a remarkable virtue worthy of true wonder. But this concept is strong with emotion and cannot be discounted. Its practical value is clear. Loyalty means to protect others from harm; the opposite is to destroy.

In the underworld of Dante's Inferno (Italian language for "Hell"), when he outlined the levels of Hell, Dante was trying to get to what constituted true Evil. He observed that there are many ways to behave wickedly, but there is also a pecking order of evil behavior, and something is at the absolute bottom, the worst of the worst. And Dante believed it was a betrayal. Betrayal is devastating. Betrayal is worse than a crime. It is worse than thievery, bribery, and even worse than murder. Betrayal destroys not just a person but the belief in the intrinsic good nature of all humans. It undermines everything we know and all we have come to hold dear to ourselves.

One human act that enables long-term peaceful cooperation between people is trust. Loyalty is the outgrowth of trust. Trust is an unbelievably powerful force in human activity; it is the basis of everything we do. Without trust, we cannot act cooperatively with others, we cannot exist peacefully, and we cannot live alongside others. Trust allows us to predict the acceptable and beneficial behavior of others. And trust is always a two-way street. Only by giving it can you gain it. If trust is to exist, trust must be given and taken, and it requires a bit of courage. To protect others and to have their back is a necessary form of trust. When someone trusts us, they know that any threat against them will be met by others.

And, of course, always "Check your 6," a recent military term. Also phrased as "watch your back," it means to be careful of what's behind you. It's a phrase adopted in civilian phraseology, where "6" refers to numbers on an imaginary clock, 12 is directly in front of you, and six is behind. Loyalty is essential in this idea because no one can be on guard against every possibility. Good friends, family, and co-workers can help you check your 6. Be situationally aware, be open to the input of others, be transparent in your dealing with others, keep your word, and remember that there are folks out there who will attempt to destroy you just because they can.

So, protect the back of others and always check your 6. Never betray your brothers or sisters.

"Do what is meaningful, not what is expedient."
— Jordan Peterson

★ **RULE 45**

Find a substitute for alcohol and dangerous drugs, and never smoke anything. Ask where you will be in the future, and you're your adventure.

Instead of starting with the obvious, finger-pointing advice that you should avoid alcohol, dangerous drugs, and smoking or quit if you are using, I will begin with an important question. What benefits do we get from indulging in them? How can we avoid something that has become commonplace, acceptable, encouraged and a mark of high fashion? We might ask first why people use alcohol and drugs. If you use them, this question is "stupid:" because the answer is in front of you and obvious. Using alcohol and dangerous drugs is fun, in vogue, chic, and exciting; it's an adventure, and they are inexpensive and easily obtained.

The problem is that alcohol and drug use has negative consequences. Use is terrible for your health, especially if you abuse them and allow their use to motivate your behavior. They leave you with destruction everywhere; terrible hangovers, failed relationships, lost jobs, destroyed motivation, and a multitude of cancers. You are likely to suffer greatly and die prematurely.

And alcohol and drugs will prevent you from learning those skills you need in social circumstances. Their consumption will make the bad things in your life worse. Alcohol and drugs destroy. The destruction might not be immediate, as often the case, but it will. It's not a matter of if they destroy; they do destroy. Sadly, alcohol and drugs destroy a large percentage of the population.

A better question to ask ourselves is, what in our life is better than alcohol, drugs, and smoking? Now that is a tricky question. We need a meaningful alternative. One could be your need to discover what is meaningful in your life and better than not having bad health and premature death. Lay out those disadvantages for yourself, be honest about them, and then the choice becomes more apparent when you see what will happen.

So, what is better? A better choice is a meaningful adventure, the instinctive need to live on the edge and discover the unknown. Replace expedient alcohol and drug use with something more adventurous that serves you better, then choosing not to use them will be more straightforward (but not easy). Ask yourself where you will be next month, in a year, or five years. The question will answer itself if you are honest. Your future is better without alcohol, dangerous drugs, and smoking.

Do you want something in your life that forces from you the best that you have? Do you have real problems to contend? You should want problems that you can solve. The growth that comes with overcoming problems is something we yearn for – stopping your alcohol, drug, and smoking habits help. Yes, it is tough; you need a solid alternative to succeed. And that alternative is an adventure. It is also a noble cause because it makes us all better.

Find a substitute for alcohol and dangerous drugs, and never ever smoke anything.

"If we could give every individual the right amount of nourishment and exercise, not too little and not too much, we would have found the safest way to health." – Hippocrates

★ **RULE 46**

Exercise daily, and stay physically and emotionally fit.

Strength. The value of human physical and mental strength is accepted across time and cultures. We respect those stronger than us, especially those who can harness their strength to protect themselves and safeguard others. There is only one method to achieve physical prowess: eating the right foods and exercising. There is no substitute, magic pill, special diet, or alternative. Building your strength takes time and discipline. And while it is not easy building strength, it is something we can all do if we put our minds to it. We must overcome the most challenging realization that proper diet and exercise take time. That is why it should be included in your daily schedule (Rule 42: Get scheduled, establish a routine). Exercise every day. There is no excuse; even when you do not feel well, there is always some exercise you can do to strengthen your muscles.

The notion that physical activity helps keep us healthy is not new. More than 1,500 years ago, Ancient Greek physician Hippocrates wrote about the dangers of too little activity (and too much food). We hear that exercise has many benefits. That is true.

Proper exercise helps control weight, combats cardiovascular disease, improves mood, boosts energy, promotes better sleep, and puts a pep in your step. It is crucial to understand that our cognitive functions start to decline at about age 25. There is a linear downward trend after that. Moderate exercise, both aerobic and anaerobic, combats that decline significantly. Those who have built a good foundation throughout their life with exercise and diet will perform better throughout their lifetime. It's never too late to start. Begin with the most basic and add to that foundation daily.

We are, however, human and are by nature averse to toil and trouble. And, we are prone to see exercise and proper diet as unnecessary or that is not worth the effort to undertake. Or maybe we will cheat only one day. At the very least, we view it as too complicated, disruptive, and inconvenient. That viewpoint is mistaken. We have limited control over our physical and emotional health, and it is up to each of us – an obligation – to take heart in properly maintaining our health.

Exercise daily, and stay physically and emotionally fit.

"All life demands struggle. Those who have everything given to them become lazy, selfish, and insensitive to the real values of life. The very striving and hard work that we so constantly try to avoid is the major building block in the person we are today."
— Pope Paul VI

★ RULE 47

Reach out and build a network. It's a good precursor to success.

We organize ourselves by talking to people. When we speak with others, we form concepts and adjust our values, usually very slightly but in agreement with the consensus of who we have in our presence. We have a choice. We can surround ourselves with folks like us, those who will parrot our thinking and behavior, or we can have people around us who force us to change for the better, to open up, and see things differently and better, some of which we can incorporate into our being. Which would you choose?

Reach out and build a social network that brings a variety of ideas to you. Add people to your circle that will alert you to opportunities. Listen closely and intently to what they have to say, make sure you understand what they say, and you will be amazed and never bored. Doing this outreach to build a network comes with risks. It exposes you to challenging ideas (many you will not like), it is difficult and tests you, and it requires courage to stand firm with your values. Your network, however, is where you can grow your character and discover new possibilities.

Construct your network with care. Put your effort into having people surround you with ideas proven successful; those who are respected for the good they've done are willing to share their thinking and have a genuine interest in helping you. The quality of the character counts more than quantity. If you cannot figure out who should be in your network, find a friend who is genuinely interested in your success and has proven a valuable member of your community and ask for help. If that person is truly of good character, they will provide a short list to start your network. Most likely, your Facebook "friends" or Twitter "followers" will not be on our list. This is the nature of a proper network. Work slowly. Two or three key people are best; that number will grow. And do them a favor so they can return a favor to you. This method helps establish trust and is a core principle for an effective network. Also, reach out to people who you too can help. Return the favor.

It takes decades to build a high-quality professional network. Those who do are very selective; each person has to show their worth. Most of your network will not be relatives, friends next door, and certainly not fly-by-night acquaintances. What is noteworthy about a functioning network is that you must personally maintain it, stay in contact, help them, be helpful, be responsive, and give them a reason to be part of your network. Those in a good network are the kind of people; if you call upon them for their help, they will come, and it matters not where they are or what they are doing; they will be there for you, ready to help. And, if they call, you will be there for them.

Reach out and build a network. It's a good precursor to success.

"If your actions inspire others to dream more, learn more, do more and become more, you are a leader." – John Quincy Adams

★ RULE 48

Be real, Be honest, Be committed, Be inspirational, and Be who you are. You can't fake it; people will see through a phony. Convince others that they too can achieve a noble goal.

Commitment is about having a strong attachment to those around you. It's about having heart in the game, the passion, sincerity, and craving to be part of something that pulls at your emotions and pulls you toward it. It's a deep thirst that's unexplainable but unmistakably with you. And this is why our primitive emotions cannot be faked. People can pick out a phony faster than the blink of an eye. We've all experienced someone who tries to be something they are not. We know who is honest and who is not. We can see through them, and it doesn't take long for them to realize they are a sham, false imitations, a charlatan. And they know we know it. This is why we've been given the advice, "Be who you are," by our family and friends since we were young. Be real ... and to be real, we must be honest, truthful, and committed to others. Fail to do so, and you are out; people will reject what you and what you say. You will not succeed by being a fake.

In his inauguration speech in 1961, President Kennedy challenged the people of America. He said, "And so, my fellow Americans: ask not what your country can do for you; ask what you can do for your country." He was saying that the best path for our future is to put our ambitions aside and work for the advancement of all citizens. Like many who succeed, he inspired us with his actions and outlook. He led from the front; he walked the talk. People are looking for leaders like him that are genuine and authentic. They don't like people telling them what they want to hear or what to do; pandering is a failed long-term strategy.

The old saying, "Do what you love," is correct. If you genuinely love what you do, and are honest with yourself and others, only then can you inspire others to action. To rally people around a noble cause is our highest calling. Those we respect the most are those we call a hero. They embody our chief values and show us how to be truly real and do those things that must be done in the face of danger. Inspire others to great achievements. Be hopeful, even in the face of discouraging setbacks and criticism. People don't follow victims, those discouraged by even small acts against them, real or imagined. Follow those who persist with hope and commitment.

Be real, be honest, be committed, be inspirational, and be who you are. You can't fake it.

"No one can please God without faith, for whoever comes to God must have faith that God exists and rewards those who seek Him" – Hebrews 11:6, The Bible

★ **RULE 49**

Remember your Faith.

Today in the West, we find that faith in God is mocked as primitive and superstitious; at its best, faith is, we are told, for the uneducated and gullible. No one who has seen the great scientific advancements in medicine, engineering, agriculture, and such, can believe in an unseen higher being. Yet, looking at people's behavior, we can see that we all operate with faith; we are always stepping into the unknown. We all take a leap of faith to exist. Yet many trivialize and demonize religious faith and those who believe in God and His principles. This resistance can be explained due at least in part to the fear of those who belittle religious faith, but that is not the point here. Faith isn't evidence-based, nor based on observation, scientific study, or finding proof in the excavations of ancient tombs or cities for religious texts, relics, or bones of the faithful.

Remember your faith. As you go out into the world, be aware that you will be tempted to forsake your beliefs and reject those who follow those religious beliefs. The temptations will be strong and without end. Holding onto your faith will test your character, and, perhaps sadly, you will find that many like you have given up their faith because of the pressure from friends, co-workers, and acquaintances, those that you respect and admire. Remember that your faith will carry you through difficult times and connect you with those doing good in their communities through church, synagogue, or mosque. The value of faith should never be underestimated. Listen to those who mock you and degrade your beliefs; they will make your faith stronger, not weaker. Listen carefully to what they say, knowing they are themselves fearful. Do the good works your religious leaders teach you. Follow the good and moral pathway, and although it is a narrow and winding way, you will forever be grateful you decided to trod upon this righteous path.

Remember your Faith.

"Education without values, as useful as it is, seems rather to make man a more clever devil." – C.S. Lewis

★ **RULE 50**

Know your values and hold them close.

When you know your values, and they are a substantial part of your being, your decisions, voluntary actions, and speech are more manageable. Values give us independence and freedom of action; they anchor us to what is real. We know where we stand, with our feet firmly planted in the predictable world. On the flip side, if you are only guided by rigid rules through memorization, without a proper understanding of why those rules exist, you will drift in your life, never knowing where you are.

Humans learn values through their embodiment in stories; the ancient way of communicating takes place in tales that are still valid today. From the time we were infants, we heard stories and demanded them from adults who surrounded us, and we would sit for hours to hear those that entertained us. That entertainment touches us deep in the recesses of our ancient minds and follows common themes of life. And we place them on a high pedestal and call them morality. Make no mistake, failing to know our values, to fail to keep them in the forefront of our consciousness, is to fail spectacularly as a social human being.

What is the highest of values? What best explains the outside world that makes sense in the easiest terms? And will those values hold up over time and ideally exist across cultures?

Our highest value is the pursuit of truth, the mapping of reality to "see" what's coming, fend off dangers, and pursue what is necessary. This idea is why words are so important, to tell the story straight, or else we will error and die or injure or lose something we need or desire. When we hold up these higher values, such as honor, integrity, truthfulness, liberty, individualism, and independence, we instinctively idolize what makes us the most human. It's the same as the hero who, with his shield and sword, kills the monster (the snake, tyrants, Dragon, or Satan) and saves great things of value (people, comrades, gold and jewels), like the ancient legends of Hercules, Odysseus, Spartacus, King Leonidas, Julius Caesar – each a martyr fighting for the common good, embodying virtues of their culture, and defender of their people.

What, then, should be the values that we hold dearest? The most obvious are those that push us closest to the truth (honor, integrity, truthfulness, liberty). Others include values implicit in our continued existence (survival, relationships, individualism and cohesion). Some values condition us to get along with others (empathy, cooperation, loyalty, and duty). These values matter and are more than a simple checklist. They are built into our culture. For example, Moses led the Israelites out of Egypt and brought down the Ten Commandments from Mount Sinai, and within the Commandments was an array of the practical values given to Moses by God. Most Western notions of law and ethics are based on these principles.

What are a few examples of American values:

1. **Liberty and Freedom.** *We can propose that freedom means being free from unfair restrictions on our ability to pursue our lives through independence and self-development.*

2. **Equality and Individualism.** *The belief that every person is special and unique. There is the expectation of privacy that we are all born equal and have equal rights under the law.*

3. **Democracy.** *Recognized early by Alexis de Tocqueville, Democracy in America was an attempt to balance liberty and equality. The basis of American beliefs is that we have respect for the law and the rights of others.*

4. **Strength and Winning.** *Americans love a winner, and they respect strength. We love sports because both of these values are at play. Likewise, in politics and international affairs, we like good competition with clear rules ... and we hate cheaters.*

5. **Family.** *The family is at the center of all we do. Americans put tremendous faith in our families, and we are fond of saying that "blood is thicker than water." We owe an allegiance to our family members and pass laws that help protect them.*

6. **Individual Responsibility.** *Americans love their ability to survive on their own without help. Those who accept government help are looked down upon as malingerers and lazy; shame is their lot.*

7. **Future Orientation, Contentment, and Life.** *This is the belief that the future holds a better time for us, especially our children. They do not look backward to the past and are less likely to hold a grudge.*

8. **Integrity and Honesty.** *These are individual characteristics that are highly valued, easily lost, and, if so, challenging to regain. Americans like to close an agreement with a handshake that confirms any contract – the basis of which is honesty and the rejection of betrayal.*

9. **Faith.** *American law and morality's history and the underlying foundation come from a solid Judeo-Christian heritage. Tolerance of and freedom of religion is the hallmark because the nation's founding came from those fleeing religious persecution.*

10. **Defender of the Helpless.** *There is a strong affinity for protecting those who cannot protect themselves. In their selfless service to their nation, Americans have been willing to risk everything to protect others from evil – tyranny, injustice, and slavery.*

As the United States continues into the 21st Century, many of our values are beginning to shift. This change is real. Yet, there is overwhelming evidence that these values will be with Americans for a long time.

Know your values and hold them close.

OUTTAKE: He was the most dangerous man I ever knew

I remember him well from my first duty assignment at Fort Benning, Georgia. The climate was hot, humid, sunny (blistering), a downpour when it rained, and the dog days of Summer were upon us. Our unit specializes in desert warfare. Our Infantry Brigade was one of the finest, most cohesive units I'd ever been a part of, and we were readying ourselves for the First Gulf War (Desert Storm). Sergeant First Class Benjamin Collins, a Vietnam veteran, was in the middle of it all. He was single, about 35 years of age and the toughest, meanest, scariest man I had ever met. Heaven forbid; he could crush you like a cockroach if you were not on his side.

At first glance, Sergeant Collins might seem to be a terrible person, somehow defiled by the war in Vietnam, turned inhuman by the terror of war and the horrors he saw. Was Sergeant Collins an angry or cruel man, a terror to Soldiers? No, just the opposite. He was the best Soldier the military had in its ranks. Some might think a more kind, empathetic, and pleasant Sergeant would be the best choice. Wrong. It takes a lion to walk among evil goers that stalk in the corners of the world. Only the strong can be relied upon to challenge those jackals. Sergeant Collins was that man.

He taught us how to defend ourselves, first with our fists and feet and then with improvised and issued weapons. We learned to defend against an enemy that outnumbered us 10 to 1. Sergeant Collins had incorporated his maliciousness, cruelty, callousness, and vindictiveness into his being, learning to control it and use it as a weapon. He was a dangerous man.

It was late August 1990. Iraq had invaded the neighboring state of Kuwait on the 2nd of the month. I was a new Captain to the unit and was being introduced to key unit members when Sergeant Collins saw me. He came over to welcome me, shook my hand (nearly crushing my fingers), looked me in the eye and said (with purpose), "Glad to have you in this man's finest Army." I smiled. He stared through me. I wondered if I'd measure up to such a man.

Later, during the Gulf War, Collins was part of the first Coalition Task Force to breach the Saudi Arabian border to engage in direct firefights with Iraqi forces. He would earn the Silver Star for bravery, two Purple Hearts for wounds he received, and a personal note from General Norman Schwarzkopf, Jr., who had heard of Sergeant Collins.

Today, this kind of man is being called "toxic" for his masculinity. They are wrong. A man like Sergeant Collins, who is very dangerous and has his emotions and his capability under voluntary control, is the embodiment of a good man. It is the weak man who is not a good man, for he cannot be relied upon to step up to stand against evil or to help protect the innocent. Not possessing strong social and emotional skills to attract women, weak men cannot compete with good men; weak are those who prey on women. Weak men are unpredictable. Weak men don't stand on moral principles. Those who are weak know they cannot defend the innocent and, when pressed, will run away like cowards to protect themselves.

Sergeant First Class Benjamin Collins was the most dangerous man I ever knew.

"You can easily judge the character of a man by how he treats those who can do nothing for him." – Malcolm S. Forbes

★ **RULE 51**

Show your respect. Respect is like the lubricant in a car engine that allows the pistons to continue firing. Without it, everything would come to a screeching halt. The Golden Rule is a practical application of the idea of respect; it tells us that we should treat others like we would like to be treated.

Growing up, we learned some simple ways of showing respect. Some were basic, like saying please and thank you. Others took a little longer to learn, such as good table manners, listening properly to what others say, keeping your promises, offering to assist others, sharing your toys, and apologizing when you are wrong.

Respect is much more than common decency (and that is important); it is the prudent judgment and recognition of someone's good deeds, authority, and their value. Respect is a deep admiration based upon noteworthy abilities, qualities, or achievements. And that means respect can be lost. If you are corrupt, weak, a cheat, a liar, a thief, if you betray others, or you are a sniveling coward, then you will garner no respect from others. That is the human way, and that will never change.

Learning how to show respect is not easy, but doing so benefits us over time. Why do we show respect? The simple reason is that doing so reaffirms that we are human and that we willingly accept the responsibility to assist our fellow citizens. Furthermore, showing respect builds trust and confidence. In this way, we can see that respect is a core building block of human existence.

As adults, we learned that showing respect reflects our good character; our interaction with others helps everyone, including our friends and family. Maturity is a trait we strive for; for practical reasons. There are also ways to show the respect we did not learn as children.

What follows are mature ways of showing respect, requiring more intellectual development.

A. **Compliment the achievements of others.** *A simple word of praise can boost morale and foster a better relationship. Compliments are one of the best and cheapest motivators. People may work for money, but compliments drive them.*

B. **When disagreeing with others, acknowledge the value of their opinion.** *Disagreements are inevitable. Focus on the facts, don't get personal, see the good, listen intently, and choose to act respectfully. You will attract more to your side by using honey rather than vinegar.*

C. **Respond to requests from others in a timely and proper fashion.** *Avoid procrastination when dealing with others; it damages relationships. Focus your efforts, and do not get distracted trying to multitask too often. Being on time with the correct response shows respect and maturity on your part.*

D. **Use humor appropriately to enliven relationships but do not tease or use sharp barbs.** *A good dose of humor goes* *a long way as a powerful tool to encourage others. However, a warning ... humor can be difficult to use correctly and cause more problems if misused. I find self-deprecating humor to be the safest and satire the riskiest.*

E. **Never gossip. Do not release confidential information.** *The worst sin a person can serve on another is betrayal. Gossip, unfounded rumor, or the release of private information is the fastest way to get yourself into trouble. This is a bad habit and hard to break. Avoid it.*

F. **Politely accept criticism as positive feedback.** *Willingly and politely receive feedback about you, and do so graciously. Listen to what others have to say. They will tell you things you may not want to hear, but they are telling you something important. It is easy to personalize what they say; don't do it.*

G. **Accept the mistakes of others.** *People aren't perfect, and you cannot assume you know their intentions. Don't be a perfectionist. Be willing to forgive and forget. We can all learn from our mistakes, and it is better to learn from the mistakes of others than your own.*

H. **Use the ideas of others and publically give them credit for their contribution.** *It's hard to underestimate the positive impact of giving credit to others. People will see you as more fair, committed, responsible, and trusted. This is genuine leadership.*

I. **Praise in public, criticize in private.** *Follow this advice to change human behavior for the better, and build understanding, empathy, and teamwork.*

J. **Look people directly in the eye and speak clearly.** *Being a good person is not based on how you look, how smart you are, or your past; it's based on your ability to candidly and clearly* *communicate. Do this by looking people in the eye and speak precisely, clearly, and without hesitation.*

K. **Don't waste people's time.** *Our time is precious; we could all spend more time with family and friends, so it is always best not to waste it. Be punctual to meetings, organized, decisive, plan ahead, keep yourself on track, anticipate obstacles, and pay attention.*

L. **Be uplifting and approachable.** *Be the person who makes another person smile, be approachable, and connect with others emotionally. That way, you will bring out the joy and meaning in others.*

M. **Know who you are talking to; know the audience.** *It's an old maxim of Toastmasters; know your audience. This knowledge is how you can become an effective communicator. It's one thing to talk with a High School student and another to be in a conversation with a University Professor.*

N. **Show extreme patience.** *It's easy to make a spur-of-the-moment decision, but waiting for the right moment to do the right thing is the goal we should strive to achieve.*

O. **Be brutally honest.** *Honesty means more than telling the truth about what you think is relevant but being straightforward and fair on everything.*

P. **Call out disrespectful behavior.** *Don't allow bad behavior to happen when you can. Stand up for the weak and innocent. Call out those who are disrespectful or ungrateful. It goes to the character of yourself. Don't be so agreeable that you are a pushover.*

Q. **Never insult, use name-calling, disparage, or belittle folks or their thoughts.** *The best way to show disrespect is to degrade someone, their family, friends, co-workers, etc. Step in the* *right direction and go out of your way to be courteous, especially when you don't want to.*

R. **Respect people, even if they don't deserve it.** *You will find this a difficult task but necessary. It is easy to underestimate others and have them come back to haunt us. Respect people and they will know it. Disrespect them, and they know that too. Do what is right and show respect to everyone.*

S. **Address people by name.** *We all want to be recognized as someone special. We like folks noticing us. The best way is to remember their names and use them often.*

T. **Never use excuses, whine, or beat around the bush.** *Stop it now. Bad habits like this might be okay for children but not for adults. Replay in your head how you behave and take voluntary actions to put an end to things that make you immature.*

U. **Share the excitement of people's wins.** *Those who genuinely believe in people and are willing to help others are also happy when folks are winners. Compliment legitimate achievements. That way, you are part of the good things people accomplish, not on the outside looking in.*

V. **Allow yourself to be visible and accessible to talk to.** *Inspire and influence. Being physically present is best; that way, people can know you care, and they can bring problems to you and talk about their wishes and desires.*

W. **Remember the small things; birthdays, major life events, spouses' names.** *These may seem minor or small to you, but they are essential. Acknowledge them; doing so makes you likable, and folks will be more open to you.*

X. **Listen first to what others have to say before expressing your ideas.** *When you express your opinion, especially early in a conversation, you influence others. Let them talk first and hear what they say; you will be appreciated more and respected for it.*

Respect all, pander to none. Show your respect. We should treat others like we would like to be treated.

"The leader must acknowledge mistakes and admit failures, take ownership of them, and develop a plan to win."
— Jocko Willink

★ RULE 52

Take ownership. Make no excuses. Don't blame any other person or any other thing. Get control of your ego.

Whatever you do, whatever you think, do something to take charge of yourself and others who are important to you. The message is that you can operate during times of tragedy, deception, and tyranny, and the good news is that you can flourish and grow. And that is a good piece of news, given that it is better than you could ever hope to wish for or that you could reasonably expect.

Pick up your responsibility; pick up the heaviest load you bear. Realize that despite your inadequacies and mistakes, you will succeed. And those who are with you will also prevail. That is really good news and is reflected in popular and interesting stories. At their core, the greatest stories ever told have the flawed hero, the one who doggedly trudges on to slay the Dragon and does so regardless of the many obstacles in his path. It is not that you are kinder, gentler, more ethical, or smarter; it is a fact of the human condition that adopting responsibility ensures you become stronger. Carrying a heavy load makes you a person with solid character, and your flaws are not what define you.

The antidote to your flaws is truth and responsibility. That is the secret to a meaningful life, and without truth and responsibility, all you have left is an inability to see the world for what it is, and your blundering will find you emptiness and suffering. Stand up and take ownership of your life; take onto yourself what you must do and what you know you must do. Use no excuse for any failure or for not doing what needs doing. See your failures as a means of learning and growth. Own those failures; they are part of what will make you better, more experienced, more motivated (because you will not want to repeat them), and wiser about the world. Do not blame others or anything; it is you who are responsible. Your goal should be to reveal to the world the overwhelming best of yourself, that part of you that can do the most good for the world.

Take ownership of your problems, and then take ownership of the solutions to solve those problems. Take ownership of your mission. Take ownership of your job, of your team (grasp the guidon), of your family, of your future, and take ownership of your life. Until you take ownership, you will always be chasing your dreams. People are starving for this message. They want to hold responsibility close to their heart because it makes them who they are and keeps them from falling into the abyss of depression and hopelessness that many folks today have wrapped around themselves.

You have no idea what might be possible for you if you got things together for what you could pursue. You don't know what is possible until you seek truth and responsibility. Go out into the world. Stand up straight. Hold your shoulders back. Do so without fear. Embrace courage. Leave your ego behind. Be humble for what you have and for those who are with you.

Take ownership of your life; there are no excuses not to.

"Only a life lived for others is a life worthwhile."
— Albert Einstein

★ **RULE 53**

Humility, it's your best friend. You're not as smart as you think, so stop acting like you know it all. And, darn it, stop taking yourself so seriously.

Humility means you are probably not as smart as you think you are. That you are a flawed person. And you know it and embrace that you are imperfect and inadequate. This is where the idea of personal responsibility comes into play. You compete with yourself to be slightly better tomorrow than you are today; you can be better in some way you can manage.

That ability to know that you can improve is the beginning of humility. Given that we are imperfect, we often ask ourselves how we can be as good as someone else. That is not the best question to ask. The better question is, can we be slightly better tomorrow than our flawed selves today? And the answer is "yes" if you can set your personal standards low enough for you to achieve them. If so, then you can be better. This is the pathway to self-improvement, and you rise above yesterday's self. This is the pathway to a meaningful life.

Be careful about what you do or say; you're probably mistaken because you are flawed and insufficient. That raises an important philosophical point that has been at the forefront of thinking for thousands of years. How do you make practical, positive changes if you don't know what you might need to know? How can you be cautious and not make mistakes? How do you do good? The answer is that you should be careful about stepping outside the area of your personal knowledge. And the solution is to start with the small things in your life.

Fix those things you can adjust within your competence. Start with those minor problems that trouble you or perhaps trouble your family. You really have to have your act together if you try to fix your family. We should acknowledge that it is hard to put yourself together and that putting your family together is really tough. Obviously, the world is more complicated than you or your family. So why do so many folks think they can save the world?

We tell kids today that they are the best in the world, that they are wonderful and can achieve anything they want. We teach them to believe they are morally superior to others, that they can do great things by thinking the right way, and they can do so easily by holding tightly onto a set of dogmatic ideas that reject religion, the freedom of speech, and any idea that runs counter to the current political thinking. This is wrong. We are raising narcissists who will be tragically disappointed in their lives and will be angry, resentful, bitter, and vindictive. Not only is this destructive personally to them, but it is also dangerous to their families and communities. They will not be a positive force to those around them. Only tragedy can result.

And while the virtue of humility is rarely discussed in our modern society, it certainly can be a noble goal. So stop taking yourself so seriously, be humble, admit your flaws and work to make yourself better each day, a little each day. Compare yourself to who you were yesterday. It should be one of our most honorable aims.

Humility is your best friend. You're not as smart as you think.

"Family is not an important thing. It's everything."
– Michael J. Fox

★ **RULE 54**

Find a mate that you can love and respect. Get married, have children, and be a couple. Never, ever forget that you're in it for the long haul. Tell the truth to your spouse. Know that marriage is the highest form of humanity. Doing this is how you find fulfillment in your life.

Why is marriage essential for you? The answer is insightful. There is no other place in your life where you can allow yourself to be honest, tell the truth with everything out in the open, and where you can develop your negotiating skills by putting them to the test. None. If you can be honest and are willing to work hard at getting along with someone and want fulfillment, then get married. And, as a bonus, marriage is the highest form of humanity possible; responsibility, honor, loyalty, selflessness, respect, and courage.

No institution, group, career, friendship, or live-in relationship demands the commitment and effort required by marriage. If you are fortunate and can find a mate you can love and respect, then marry that person. And despite those flaws you both bring to the table, you are on the only path to a good life. And, if fortune shines upon you, you will also have children and raise them together. There is nothing more rewarding and fulfilling than marriage with children.

A marriage is a vow, a voluntary contract to stay together and support your partner no matter what the world brings your way. "From this day forward, for better, for worse, for richer, for poorer, in sickness and in health…" the marriage vow is a sacred promise – a practical and moral promise – that is sworn with family and friends present and in the presence of God, and is not meant to be broken. The vow is not a conditional declaration; it is forever, "till death do us part," a literal and symbolic joining of two people. If you commit to it this way, only then can you will be fulfilled. Don't let others talk you into thinking the words of the vow are conditional. If you are not deadly serious or don't have the guts to do what it takes to hold the marriage together, then marriage is not for you, and you will never get fulfillment. You could get some fulfillment by writing poetry, participating in a glee club, or joining a church or synagogue. If you still want love, get a dog. Unfair? Yeah, that's why marriage is about adopting responsibility. This is the way toward thriving and love.

My wife's idea of marriage is straightforward; you're in it for the long haul. "I'm not leaving you, ever, no matter what." We are all full of liabilities and weaknesses, and only through marriage can we bond together so that there is no "out" and that marriage union forces us to sort out our problems. There is no running away; that is the coward's way. If you were able to run away, you cannot tell that person the truth. The marriage forces you to tell the truth. And it forces you to negotiate with your spouse over every sort of thing; mundane daily chores, in-laws, joint careers, where you are going to live, and whether to have children (and you should have children). You can spar with a good spouse because you both have hard problems to solve. It takes both of you to find a solution.

Some folks need this level of seriousness to push them to sort things out. You either force yourselves to straighten out the relationship, or you will suffer for it for the rest of your life. Without that bond, there are things you will never learn because you will avoid them. Unless you've made a serious, lifetime commitment, one that you are not going to back out of, you're not going to take the relationship with the seriousness necessary to make it of the highest quality and sustainability across your lifetime.

Alternative to marriage like domestic partnerships, cohabitation, starter marriages (aka "trial" marriages – yep, there is such a thing), open marriages, friendship (aka companionship) marriages, and safety marriages (marrying for money) don't work out too well. The notion that these forms of relationships will satisfy you in the long run is laughable. Okay, your call.

I had a friend once from a small town south of Chicago who didn't come into his marriage with much honesty (he'd been married twice before and didn't tell his fiancé). He spent time hanging out and drinking with a few of his girlfriends from his past. I'll let your imagination run free, and you are right. The typical female does not appreciate this kind of behavior from their groom. Open marriages are supposed to work only if both agree to the arrangements (oh, they don't work well anyway). Dennis (not his real name) and I spoke about his outside activities because he called for advice. I told him that his philandering was inappropriate, stupid, and wrong. Stop it now was good advice. Just imagine his surprise when one day he came home to a certified letter containing divorce papers. Dennis realized that he would soon be divorced, and his behavior was to blame. The chances of getting another lady of that caliber in that town were not so good. Oddly, our relationship degenerated badly after that. Some people are beyond helping with the advice they need.

If you can get to know someone long enough to know that you two can tell the truth with each other, be honest, communicate, and negotiate. If you can do that, marriage is the right place for you. Find your mate, marry, have children, and hold your marriage together. That is the only way you can be the best you can be and find fulfillment.

Find a mate that you can love and respect. Get married, have children, and be a couple.

"That which you most need will be found where you least want to look." – Carl Jung

★ **RULE 55**

Find the Dragon. Go into the unknown voluntarily and put yourself together properly.

"Be true to yourself."

"Just do your best."

"I'm okay; you're okay."

No! Wrong! You are far more than you are; you are much better than you could ever believe you could be. This is the old idea of personal responsibility; compete with yourself to better yourself, find truth where you can (and don't be easily misled), stand up for yourself, face your fears, and be prepared to go places you might not want to go. Find the Dragon. It's a helluva lot better to find the Dragon in its lair than waiting for it to come and eat you.

If you want to put yourself together properly, you will find what you need where you least want to look. We see this idea in the many religious stories where the Devil tempts us with wealth, power, and luxury, the very things that lure those of us with weak character. The idea is deep, ancient, and wise – perhaps that is why it persists so strongly.

We must go out into the world and face reality to gain what it offers. It is frightening but necessary if we desire to make things better. It pushes us to our very limits, and why not? If we are not pushed to our limits, there will be nothing of value to gain. You don't get one without the other; you don't get support from the world without the prospect of experiencing fear.

There is a choice that is complex and challenging, and you do not have the freedom to ignore making a choice. This is a very strange, primeval idea with great wisdom attached to it. If you don't deal with your problems and challenges, they will become bigger and potentially destroy you. Ignoring those things you know you need to do will ultimately harm you. This is a lesson we all know but also choose to ignore more than we should.

There's an old blues music idea that you meet the Devil at the crossroads. This idea is really exciting. Imagine yourself standing at a crossroads (a metaphor for making a decision). You can go one way or another. Even no decision to not chose a direction is still a decision. You will find your greatest challenges, fears, and opportunities at the crossroads. Do you choose willful ignorance, envy, victimhood, succumbing to temptations, and vindictiveness? Or do you choose the pursuit of the good, truth, honor, the noble cause, and responsibility? You have the free will to choose.

Which way will you go at the crossroads?

Find the Dragon. Go into the unknown voluntarily and put yourself together properly. Choose wisely.

"If opportunity doesn't knock, build a door." – Milton Berle

★ **AFTERWARD**

A Few Things to Think About

This book will not tell you how to live. But it will tell you about what you can do to live properly. By bearing the greatest burden, by looking at what you most fear, and by holding your head up and looking people in the eye, you can live a good life.

So, don't overestimate yourself, but don't underestimate who you could be. That is a far better way of thinking about your life. We have heard a message from social scientists and philosophers – at least since the 1960s – that we should be content with ourselves and be happy the way we are. We can feel better, they say, by building up our self-esteem. These scientists have it wrong. You are nowhere near what you could be, not even close.

I have a far more optimistic message.

"You ain't seen nuttin' yet." ... now, that's the right message. You have so much influence as an individual if only you can get your act together. It is unbelievable what you can do. You have so much influence as a person. You have all the power, where you are right now, to put things right around you. You may not believe it, but it is true.

Start now, develop a noble vision of who you could be and put that into practice; develop some discipline, study the great works of the past, learn to read, write, speak, and think and do them all with seriousness in your heart. You will be unbeatable. The way to do this is to do something not often done. Put your emphasis on individual responsibility. The right way to do this is to start with yourself. Develop a worthwhile vision for your life. Start thinking about what that would look like if you could be who you could be. If you could be the person that you would admire, who would that person be? That is maturity, that is being a grown-up, and that is being a person anyone can admire.

You also have to act in a way that also works for your family; otherwise, your family is going to have problems and cause you and them all sorts of misery and grief. And not just your family today but also your family in the future. And your community. This idea means you have to set your aspirations so that your aims serve you in the broadest sense over a long period and also serve your family and community.

Remember, you are responsible for your destiny. How would that look if you wanted to be the noblest person you could be, someone who was adopting the maximum amount of responsibility? You will need a strategy to put that into place. That is how you change things properly and do the least harm. It should be an individual focus – a personal set of ideas that stresses and forces individual responsibility. One of the things required is that you need a meaningful counterbalance to the tragedies of life. Otherwise, you just suffer foolishly, and worse, you tend to make people around you suffer the same way. The way you find that meaning is by adopting as much responsibility as you can. Are you living up to your potential? You will never know the answer to that question until you take on the tremendous load of responsibility.

Set yourself a serious challenge. It takes the challenge to pull your mature, developed self out of you and to motivate you to rid yourself of all the weaknesses and personality flaws you have accumulated. A noble goal is a very good way of beginning. The truth is each of us has enough potential and character. If we can contend with it in a noble way and rise above it, then we can make the world a better place for our family, our community, one small step at a time and ourselves. And, we can constrain the evil, at least in our own hearts and have a positive effect on those around us as a consequence. That does make things better, and we can do it. That is where the good life is to be found.

The good life, which goes along with the adoption of great responsibility, is the antidote to the suffering and arbitrariness that life brings. You need a reason to get out of bed in the morning, especially when things are not going to be great in your life.

Tell the truth, especially to yourself. You know what is wrong with you if you ask yourself seriously. Start today, don't wait; begin by putting your own house in order. Now, you can begin your day with a smile and with the knowledge you know the way ahead.

Remember that you should be better than you are, not because you're worse than other people, but because you're not everything you should be. Be more than you ever thought you could be.

"Once you learn to read, you will be forever free." - *Frederick Douglas*

APPENDIX:

Good Books to read!

You are molded and shaped by culture; consequently, you are a historical creature. But culture is often corrupt, oppressive, unjust, and tyrannical. Implicit in your being is the necessity to breathe new life into the ancient culture that has had its way with you. This is the hero and the Dragon metaphor, where the hero slays the fire-breather Dragon (old culture), rescues the princess (the new culture) and lives happily ever after (despite his flaws and challenges of the new culture).

This story means that you have to face what you fear most. And when you do that, you will reinvigorate the culture and rid it of its corruption and its tyranny (even if a small amount). You have to do this before you can become who you could be. Culture may be a straight jacket but also protective and benevolent.

Rejuvenating your culture is accomplished by adopting responsibility for your own being and then acting as a moral agent in the culture. This is why you become educated. Read books, read these books of great authors. Read them carefully, focus your attention on the words and meaning, absorb what the authors have written, and think about what they tell us about you. They will change your life, and you will become something greater than you are now.

I have now run an online leadership blog for nearly a decade. There are more than 100 books on my blog's Reading List. This shortlist contains books that rise above the others. Some are genuinely terrifying. They all possess wisdom that opens our eyes to evil and good, giving deep insight into human behavior. I believe a noble person must be capable of seeing and understanding evil. For it is those who are good that will unambiguously take a righteous stand against evil.

1. **12 Rules for Life, Jordan Peterson, 2018**
Renowned psychologist Jordan B. Peterson answers the most difficult questions about what makes a successful life. He does this by combining the hard-won truths of ancient tradition with the stunning revelations of cutting-edge scientific research.

2. **1984, George Orwell, 1949**
The book is a dystopian novel that centers on the consequences of totalitarianism, mass surveillance, and the repressive regimentation of people. The novel examines the role of truth and facts in politics and how they are manipulated.

3. **Antifragile, Nassim Nicholas Taleb, 2012**
Taleb discusses how to gain from disorder and chaos while being protected from fragilities and adverse events. Antifragile provides a blueprint for how to behave – and thrive – in a world we don't understand.

4. **Art of War, Sun Tzu, 5th century BC**
This book is an ancient Chinese military treatise that studies the anatomy of political states in conflict. The writings apply to many fields, well outside the military.

5. **As a Man Thinketh, James Allen, 1903**
The underlying premise is that noble thoughts make a noble person, while lowly thoughts make a miserable person. In his

book, James Allen reveals how our thoughts determine reality; our underlying beliefs shape our character, our health and appearance, our circumstances, and our destinies.

6. Brave New World, Aldous Huxley, 1932

The book explores the negatives of an ostensibly prosperous world in which everyone appears content and satisfied with excessive carnal pleasures. Yet, this stability is only achieved by sacrificing freedom in its true sense and the idea of personal responsibility.

7. Beyond Good and Evil, Friedrich Nietzsche, original 1886

It has become increasingly clear that Nietzsche's writings are among the most profound and visionary sources we have for acquiring a philosophical understanding of the roots of 20th-century culture.

8. Crime and Punishment, Fyodor Dostoevsky, original 1866

This book is a novel that follows the mental anguish and moral dilemmas of Rodion Raskolnikov, an impoverished ex-student in Saint Petersburg who plans to kill an unscrupulous pawnbroker. The book demonstrates the struggles over the guilt and horror of the consequences of our deeds.

9. Extreme Ownership, Jocko Willink, 2019

Extreme Ownership is a mindset that applies to everything you do. These principles can be applied to any relationship or walk of life; they are simple enough for anyone to understand and broad enough to use in any situation. The book focuses on taking aim at being a great leader and that you must have extreme internal motivation to accomplish it.

10. Gulag Archipelago (3 volumes). Aleksandr Solzhenitsyn, 1973 – 75

History and memoir of life in the Soviet Union's prison camp system by Russian novelist Solzhenitsyn. He used the word archipelago as a metaphor for the camps scattered through the sea of civil society like a chain of islands extending "from the Bering Strait almost to the Bosporus."

11. Man's Search for Meaning, Viktor E. Frankl, 1946

Frankl relates the severe conditions in the Nazi concentration camp. Those without any purpose seemed to perish. Those that had developed purpose and meaning in the harsh conditions got out of bed every morning to face another unbearable day.

12. Ordinary Men, Christopher R. Browning, 1998

This book tells how ordinary men, not necessarily anti-Jewish, could turn into mass murderers. And we arrogantly ignore that fact and risk repeating the same mistake today.

13. The Power of Positive Thinking, Norman Vincent Peale, 1952

The book starts with the "will." Does one really want to get better? The techniques and thought processes taught in this book won't magically remove dire circumstances. However, it can change your approach to them, which can cause you to reverse the self-imposed ones. It starts with the desire to change your own life.

I saved the best, most useful, most popular religious anthology ever written for last:

14. The Holy Bible

The Bible is a saga that spans all of human history. It contains the most incredible stories of humans and gives us answers to the most fundamental questions of our existence. It is about God's plans and purposes for fellowship with all people on Earth.

The Author

Lieutenant Colonel Douglas R. Satterfield, December 2004, Baghdad, Iraq

Retiring in 2014, Brigadier General Doug Satterfield entered the U.S. Army in 1974 on active duty as a Private. After completing his enlisted service, he attended college and was commissioned as an Officer. He retired after 40 years of service.

Doug is an author, American patriot, family man, Christian, Boy Scout leader, and advocate for Veterans. He lives with his wife Nancy and Bella, their yellow Labrador Retriever. They have four children and five grandchildren.

The End

(The end of this book, but the beginning of your life)

.

www.ingramcontent.com/pod-product-compliance
Lightning Source LLC
Chambersburg PA
CBHW070806050426
42452CB00011B/1917